IN SEARCH OF
SWALLOWS & AMAZONS
Arthur Ransome's Lakeland

Roger Wardale

Published by Sigma Leisure – an imprint of
Sigma Press, Stobart House, Pontyclerc, Penybanc Road
Ammanford, Carmarthenshire SA18 3HP

British Library Cataloguing in Publication Data
A CIP record for this book is available from the British Library

ISBN: 978-1-85058-839-9

Typesetting and Design by: Sigma Press, Ammanford, Carmarthenshire

Cover: Coniston Old Man from Kelly Hall Farm

Photographs: Roger Wardale, except where indicated

Printed by: Bell & Bain Ltd, Glasgow

Disclaimer: the information in this book is given in good faith and is believed to be correct at the time of publication. No responsibility is accepted by either the author or publisher for errors or omissions, or for any loss or injury howsoever caused. Only you can judge your own fitness, competence and experience

Acknowledgements

The greatest pleasure I have had in the preparation of this book, originally published as *Arthur Ransome's Lakeland* in 1986, came from the help and encouragement which I received from so many people.

My special thanks must go to John Bell, who on behalf of the Arthur Ransome Estate, allowed me to select so freely amongst Ransome's unpublished diaries, notebooks, sketch-books and letters, as well as allowing me to reproduce extracts from the stories.

The late Tony Colwell of Jonathan Cape, Ransome's publisher, encouraged me to write *Arthur Ransome's Lakeland* and was unstinting with his help and support.

The major collection of Ransome papers is held at the Brotherton Library at the University of Leeds and I am grateful for the co-operation of Christopher Sheppard and his staff, particularly Ann Farr whose knowledge and help over the years has proved invaluable. The other notable collection is at Abbot Hall Art Gallery and Museum in Kendal, and I am indebted to Mary Burkett and Gillian Riding for their help. I am also pleased to acknowledge that permission has been given to reproduce material from both collections.

David McNiell, Map Room Assistant at the Royal Geographical Society, was very helpful in supplying me with large scale maps. It was always a pleasure to visit Kendal and Windermere Libraries where the reference librarians were invariably busy, but always helpful.

I was very fortunate to meet all the people to whom, when they were children, Ransome had made his gift of *Swallows and Amazons*. I am grateful to Taqui Altounyan, Susie Villard, Mavis Guzelian, Roger Altounyan and Brigit Sanders for sharing their memories of those far-off days in Coniston and Aleppo, and talking to me of the impact that the amazing success of the books had upon their lives.

My thanks are due to Ted Alexander, who has always been most helpful.

Everyone writing about Ransome during the last thirty years owes a debt to Hugh Brogan and Christina Hardyment, who each published a major work to coincide with Ransome's centenary in 1984.

I would also like to express my appreciation to Jim Andrews, Sheila and Rebecca Barton, Elizabeth Berry, John Berry, Helen and Sheila Caldwell, John Cowen, Janet Gnosspelius, Desmond and Dick Kelsall, Adrian Murray, Charlotte Ryton, Dave Sewart, Lin and Suzannah Strange, and Alan Wilkins.

In preparing this edition, I must thank Christina Hardyment and Dave Sewart (successors to John Bell), and Diana Sparkes and David Jones for making available their research. The Jonathan Cape-Arthur Ransome archive is held at the University of Reading and I am pleased to record appreciation for their help, and also to the Random House Group Ltd for permission to quote from the letters in the collection.

Every effort has been made to contact copyright holders and I offer sincere apologise to any that I have been unable to reach.

Notes on the Photographs

Almost all my photographs have been taken over a period of fifty years using various Leica cameras and 35mm and 90mm lenses. One exception is the print of a possible North Pole, which came from a single frame of an 8mm cine film. My intention has always been, so far as it was possible, to photograph a scene as Ransome knew it and described in his books. Most of the photographs have been chosen to fit a particular extract from the text and another group shows some of Ransome's Lake District homes.

Unless otherwise credited, all photographs are by the author.

Roger Wardale

Contents

Introduction

The small girl balanced precariously on top of a rock by the island on Coniston Water, and called out, 'Look at me, Mummy. I'm on Titty's rock!'

A few feet above her, sitting on an outcrop of rock that overlooked the island's little harbour, a stranger picnicking with her own children, smiled to herself and said nothing. The amused onlooker knew just what the child meant, for she was Titty Guzelian whom Arthur Ransome had 'borrowed' for the classic adventure story that he wrote originally for her family. The girl on the rock was slipping between make-believe and reality, as readers have been doing ever since Ransome began to conjure magic in *Swallows and Amazons*. Such is the power of the imagery in Ransome's books that for more than seventy years people have gone searching for the 'secret' places that have attracted them, convinced that they are to be found somewhere. In my exploration, I have climbed the waterfall as Titty and Roger did in *Swallowdale*, peered through the glassless window of 'The Dogs' Home' like Dorothea in *The Picts and the Martyrs*, and explored the tunnel in search of Slater Bob's Mine. Nothing, however, quite compares with the thrill of bringing a small boat into Wild Cat Island's hidden harbour.

My introduction to Arthur Ransome came through listening to Derek (Uncle Mac) McCulloch's wonderful readings on BBC Children's Hour before I was old enough to read the stories for myself. Once I had tackled *The Big Six* on my own, I began to devour the others as soon as they appeared on the shelves of the local library. I kept renewing each book until a fresh one arrived, so that I was never without one or other of the series. In those gloomy days of post-war austerity, Ransome's books were at the height of their popularity. I read books by other writers; Malcolm Saville, David Severn, and Garry Hogg in particular, but there was something special about Ransome's stories, some extra quality, that they made me feel sure the lake must really exist. I was puzzled, however, by the maps in Badderley's *Lake District* for none of the real lakes looked the right shape.

Finally, after much pleading on my part, my mother raised the money by doing a little B&B and took me to Bowness-on-Windermere, which we chose because, on the map, it looked as if it might be Rio. I remember *The Lakes Express* from Euston crawling at a walking pace all the way from Oxenholm to Windermere in steady drizzle, before finally arriving two hours late. A fine rain was still falling the following morning when we walked down to Bowness Bay and into the make-believe world of the Swallows and Amazons. A steamer was about to leave the pier, rowing boats were milling about in the rain, and we could see past the wooden boat sheds to Long Island. We sat in a shelter overlooking the bay for hours, and the rain did not matter one bit! When at last it stopped, we went on a fruitless search for Holly Howe. We had more success to the north of Bowness

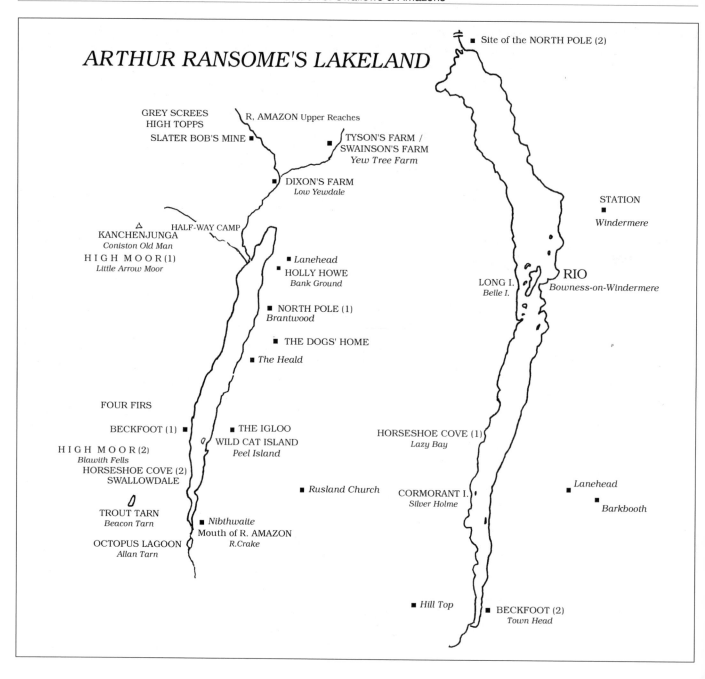

ARTHUR RANSOME'S LAKELAND

Site of the NORTH POLE (2)

GREY SCREES
HIGH TOPPS
SLATER BOB'S MINE ■

R, AMAZON Upper Reaches

■ TYSON'S FARM /
SWAINSON'S FARM
Yew Tree Farm

■ DIXON'S FARM
Low Yewdale

STATION
■
Windermere

△
KANCHENJUNGA   HALF-WAY CAMP
Coniston Old Man
H I G H M O O R (1)
Little Arrow Moor

■ *Lanehead*
■ HOLLY HOWE
Bank Ground

■ NORTH POLE (1)
Brantwood

■ THE DOGS' HOME

■ *The Heald*

LONG I.
Belle I.

RIO
Bowness-on-Windermere

FOUR FIRS

BECKFOOT (1) ■   ■ THE IGLOO
WILD CAT ISLAND
Peel Island

HORSESHOE COVE (1)
Lazy Bay

H I G H M O O R (2)
Blawith Fells
HORSESHOE COVE (2)
SWALLOWDALE

■ *Rusland Church*

CORMORANT I. ■
Silver Holme

■ *Lanehead*
■ *Barkbooth*

TROUT TARN
Beacon Tarn

■ *Nibthwaite*
Mouth of R. AMAZON
R.Crake

OCTOPUS LAGOON
Allan Tarn

■ *Hill Top*

■ BECKFOOT (2)
Town Head

when we followed Rayrigg Road to the bay now occupied by Windermere Steamboat Museum. There, moored in the bay, was the houseboat. I took a photograph, and just in case it did not 'come out', we sat on the wall and drew it.

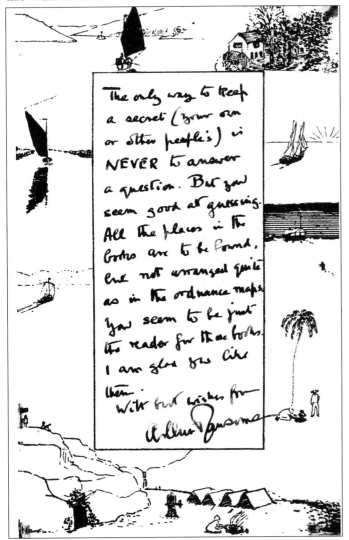

Ransome's illustrated card

I wrote to Mr Ransome and asked if the boat I had seen really was the houseboat, and if he was Captain Flint. 'Please would you tell me where all the other places are,' I added, 'so that on my next holiday I could visit them.' After a while, he responded with the celebrated reply he sent to all such inquirers:

> The only way to keep a secret (your own and other people's) is NEVER to answer a question. But you seem good at guessing. All the places in the books are to be found, but not arranged quite as in the ordnance maps. You seem to be just the reader for those books. I am glad you like them.
>
> With best wishes from
> Arthur Ransome

'All the places in the books are to be found …' I felt as if Arthur Ransome had issued a challenge and I made up my mind to be equal to it – although it was to be another six years before I had the opportunity to return to the Lake District. The photograph of the houseboat came out very well and this started my photographic record of the setting of the Swallows and Amazon books. I photographed the boatsheds in Rio Bay and then I had the good fortune to discover the secret of Peel Island from Collingwood's *The Lake Counties*. In the books, the question of essential supplies was answered by the presence of some nearby farm, but identifying the various farms, was a difficult problem. In 1966 I wrote again, telling Mr Ransome of my collection of photographs and asking for more help. To my surprise, Evgenia replied:

> My husband has been a very sick man for the last six or seven years. Lately his health has deteriorated still further. He is in Hospital at present and quite unable to deal with his correspondence.
>
> The Lake District is the background of the *Swallows and Amazons* stories but it is rather more like it used to be in the days of Dr Ransome's own early childhood than it is today. He had deliberately mixed up his topog-

raphy and rolled up into one lake, Coniston and Windermere so as to include the best features of both; he called Coniston Old Man Kanchenjunga, Bowness-on-Windermere Rio, one of the tiny (I believe nameless) islets in the southern half of Windermere Cormorant Island and made Wild Cat Island partly from Blake Holme on Windermere and partly from Peel Island on Coniston; except for these few you will not be able to find 'exact' spots though you will find coves, bays and promontories closely enough resembling those described in the books if you drift along the shores in a boat and scenery like that of High Tops *(sic)*or High Moor if you walk on Furness fells.

The houses and farms were put onto *Swallows and Amazons* map just as and where the stories demanded them and the names like Atkinson's, Dixon's or Tyson's given to them because these are the typical and most common for the district. And while almost any old traditional farm would do for the purpose of your photography – the difficulty is to find them.

Since the end of the war the District has been in a fever of pulling down, converting, modernising and generally disfiguring old buildings and replacing the farms with factory-like structures and replacing decent houses and cottages with suburban villas and bungalows all glaring with acres of so-called picture windows and bristling with forests of TV aerials.

With the roads being continually straightened and widened, with unsightly camping and caravan sites being developed on all sides, with the ever increasing numbers of motor boats on the lakes and the hoards of the wrong kind of tourist visiting the District nowadays it will be soon difficult to imagine that it has ever been as quiet and peaceful as Dr Ransome described it in his books.

Yours sincerely
Evgenia Ransome
Mrs Arthur Ransome

All this was rather misleading. There are several locations fitting their description, although others seem to have been a mixture, like the fictional lake itself. Dixon's, Tyson's and Swainson's have characteristics that enable them to be identified with farms in the Yewdale valley that Ransome knew well as a young man. It is quite possible that Evgenia did not know of the connection.

Since that first holiday I have returned to the Lake District time and time again and spent hours 'Ransome-hunting' or revisiting favourite haunts in search of better photographs, the best of which appear in this book.

In 1969 Taqui Altounyan's childhood memoir *In Aleppo Once* included a chapter which gave some details of the origin of the stories and the children involved. Ransome's centenary in 1984 brought the first of the related literature, Hugh Brogan's biography and Christina Hardyment's *Arthur Ransome and Captain Flint's Trunk*. My own book, *Arthur Ransome's Lakeland* appeared in 1986 and its companion, *Arthur Ransome's East Anglia,* two years later. The incomplete 13th Swallows and Amazons book, *Coots in the North,* together with some short stories and a couple of chapters from his unfinished Victorian novel, was also published in 1988. I published a book about Ransome's sailing life, named after his favourite yacht, *Nancy Blackett,* in 1991, and Claire Kendall-Price's book of walks, *In the Footsteps of the Swallows and Amazons,* came out in 1993.

I thought I had captured all the photographic images I was ever likely to find, when I took part in the Soundscape production *On the Trail of Swallows and Amazons* for BBC Radio Four, with Claire Kendall Price. Together with four young enthusiasts, we stayed at Holly Howe for four hectic days in the autumn of 2000, while we went in search of Wild Cat Island, Dixon's Farm, Swainson's Farm, Swallowdale, Rio, Slater Bob's Mine, The Dogs' Home and Low

Ludderburn, the cottage where Ransome wrote his stories. We met present day charcoal burners and sang shanties in the houseboat with Arthur Ransome Lupton, Ransome's nephew. At Yew Tree Farm near Coniston we came across a corner which corresponded exactly with Ransome's illustration of Mary Swainson darning Roger. We had identified Swainson's Farm at last!

In preparing this enlarged edition I have turned to primary sources in presenting an account of the origins of the Lake Country books, their characters and their setting. A new chapter traces the trials and tribulations that accompanied their creation.

Memories are at best selective and subject to recollection 'with advantages'. I have looked for contemporary written evidence wherever possible. The Brotherton Collection at the University of Leeds holds the diaries of Ransome and his wife as well as his pocket books. In addition there are 300 letters that he wrote to his mother and dozens of drafts for his letters, as well as correspondence from his friends accumulated over the years. Ransome wrote several accounts of the origin of *Swallows and Amazons* and drafts of these survive. There are also hundreds of uncatalogued photographs and negatives in the Brotherton Collection. The Abbot Hall Gallery in Kendal holds the sketchbooks, working notes, hand-made Christmas cards from friends and admirers, and yet more photographs, as well as the journal of his lifelong friend, Dora Collingwood.

Unfortunately there are gaps in the sequence of letters to his mother, and none of the diaries for the crucial months before he started to write *Swallows and Amazons* contain much of value. Ransome's later accounts of the source of *Swallows and Amazons* differ depending when they were prepared. "How Swallows and Amazons Came to be Written" seems to have been composed quite soon after publication in

Arthur Ransome was an enthusiastic fisherman who tied his own trout and salmon flies. (Author's collection)

Captain Flint's Houseboat. The original photograph of *Esperance* that started my quest more than 50 years ago.

England with the object of introducing the book to American readers. Ransome returned to the subject again shortly afterwards with a piece he called "Letter to a Friend", that he did not publish, and finally, when working on his autobiography thirty years later, he wrote an account that was edited out of the text when it was finally published in 1976.

Some of the considerable correspondence between Ransome and his publisher exists at the University of Reading Library, but there are many gaps.

Ransome claimed that by writing children's books he was able to have the best of childhood over again. He might have added that by writing about the Lake District he was able to revisit the country he had called 'paradise'.

Chapter One

Arthur Ransome and the Lake District

Although both his father and his grandfather came from the Lake District, Arthur Ransome was born and grew up in Leeds where his father was Professor of History at the Yorkshire College (now the University of Leeds). Not everyone can be born in the Lake District and so to make amends, in the spring of 1884 Cyril Ransome carried his young son, still only a few weeks old, to the summit of Coniston Old Man. The professor was essentially a countryman. He was a keen field naturalist, and a good shot, but above all he loved fishing and he had a passion for the Lake Country.

From about the age of seven until Cyril Ransome's death in 1897, young Arthur spent the long summer vacations with his family at Swainson's Farm in the hamlet of High Nibthwaite near the foot of Coniston Water. Swainson's Farm lies at the very foot of the fells, only a couple of minutes from the shore of the lake. The fells themselves are gentle and covered in bracken. The whole family thought it a 'magical place'. For almost three months of every year they became Lake Country folk. The professor fished and his wife painted her watercolours, and their absorption left the four children 'free in paradise'. Sometimes they all rowed a mile up the lake to Peel Island and picnicked, while their father drifted along the shore in the boat and was so engrossed in his fishing that he forgot to eat his sandwiches. In his autobiography Ransome recalls making friends with the animals, the postman, gamekeepers, charcoal-burners, fishermen and the odd poacher or two. The children helped with the hay making, turned the butter churn and tickled trout under the tiny bridge. When at last it was time to go, Arthur returned to Leeds carrying a large cardboard box with partitions that contained caterpillars, newts and lizards, or jars of minnows destined for the aquarium.

Those timeless days spent on the lake or in the pebbly shallows by the boat landing became the stuff of dreams, and the dream was to remain with Ransome throughout his life. Years later, whilst in Russia, he recalled with longing, the sight of the Coniston hills across the water from Nibthwaite.

Lake District summers have more than their share of wet days, and on such days it was Mrs Ransome's habit to read aloud to the children, while the professor, unable to fish, spent his time writing history books. In his autobiography Ransome says that his mother enjoyed reading aloud and read extremely well. He mentions Kipling's *Jungle Book*, *Lorna Doone*, *The Hunting of the Snark*, *Alice* and books by Charles Kingsley and Andrew Lang. Their own special book was the Norse saga *Thorstein of the Mere* by W.G. Collingwood that was set in the nearby valley of the River Crake and 'their' island.

Back home in Leeds, Arthur had a succession of

The farm at Nibthwaite where the Ransome family spent their summer holidays.

tutors. He was a lively, sensitive and mischievous little boy, who with his friend Ric Eddison, contrived to make life almost unbearable for the unfortunate young men employed to teach them. When he was nine he was sent to prep school at The Old College in Windermere. His undiscovered short-sight meant that he was considered a duffer at games, and because the school was one where the academic work was inadequate and boxing and cricket dominated school life, Arthur became the butt of both boys and teachers. The miseries of school could only be forgotten briefly when he went for Sunday lunch to his Great Aunt Susan, who lived at The Terrace above Windermere railway station. What small pleasures

The Old College, Windermere. (Author's collection)

were to be had at school came from his love of the countryside. On formal school walks he used to linger behind for as long as he dared in order to listen to the music of the beck as it tumbled through the woods towards the lake. One of his letters home told of his success as a conjuror and asked for some rats or mice in a cage as 'a lot of the boys are getting pets'. Once he made a token attempt to ran away, but he did not get far before being brought back exhausted by the Ullswater coach.

Ransome's abiding memory of his days at The Old College was of the Great Frost of 1895, when Windermere froze for a month, and the boys were allowed to spend day after day on the ice. They would pile their food on a toboggan and run it down the hill into Bowness. Arthur had learnt to skate at Leeds and he suddenly found himself in the unfamiliar position of being better than the other boys, many of whom had never skated before. He watched an ox being roasted in Bowness Bay and a coach and horses criss-crossing the ice-bound lake. On Sundays, train-loads of day-trippers from Manchester and Liverpool poured out of the station and down the hill until it was estimated that there were more then 20,000 people on the ice. Ice-yachts skimmed over the ice, keeping well away from the crowds gathered near the bands that accompanied the figure-skaters. The boys stayed on until it was dark, when the bay was alight with lanterns and torches.

The holidays at Nibthwaite continued until his father's early death from complications that had developed after he had a fall whilst fishing in the dark. Arthur managed to scrape into his father's public school and while he was at Rugby he had the good fortune to come under the influence of a master who discovered that he hoped for a literary career, and actively encouraged him. Since writing was considered a precarious career, Mrs Ransome who thought that her eldest son should settle for a steady job, did not welcome this encouragement. Arthur had been reading since the age of four, and his first book, about a desert island, was completed when he was still only eight. By the time he was seventeen he had a very good idea of what he wanted to do with his life, but first he had to get through university. He had been studying science for less than two terms at the Yorkshire College, when he came across the *Life of William Morris*. The ideals of the art and craft movement appealed to Ransome and he made up his mind to put aside what could only be, for him, a second-best career in order to follow his ambition to become a writer. After persuading his mother to allow him to go to London, he took a job as office boy for a publishing firm.

At first there was little opportunity for writing, but when he joined the Unicorn Press. in order to have more free time, he began to put pen to paper. Most of his early outpourings ended up on the fire, and on one occasion he had so much to burn that he set his mother's chimney alight. He was encouraged by some early sales to magazines, and in 1903, as soon as he had been with the Unicorn Press long enough to be given a holiday, he headed north on the overnight train for Coniston.

Ransome booked himself into Bank House in the village and paid £1 for his week's lodging. A chance meeting with W.G. Collingwood, who found him lying on a rock in the middle of the Coppermines Beck, had a profound effect upon his life. 'Are you alive, young man?' asked Collingwood, for the body on the rock appeared dead. On learning that Ransome had been trying to write poetry, he invited him to call at his home at Lanehead on the other side of Coniston Water. Ransome and Collingwood had met while both families were picnicking on Peel Island in 1895, but it took all week for him to summon enough courage to take up the invitation, but on his last evening he presented himself at Lanehead only to find the family entertaining friends to dinner. In spite of his untimely arrival he was warmly welcomed and told that next time he was in the north, he should call as soon as he arrived at Coniston.

Back in London, Ransome left the Unicorn Press and took lodgings in Chelsea. He was still only nineteen, but by selling articles to magazines, he managed to make enough money – or nearly enough – to live. The following year as soon as he arrived in Coniston, he was invited to stay with the Collingwoods, who seemed to Ransome to be the living embodiment of William Morris's ideal. W.G. Collingwood was a writer, painter, antiquary and archaeologist. Ransome called him 'The Skald' in recognition of his

Lanehead, beside Coniston Water was the family home of the Collingwoods.

Norse scholarship, and said, 'There never was a man who did so much for other people'. His wife was a painter of portrait miniatures. Of all his friendships, that of the Collingwood family was the most important to his career as a writer. Above all, they gave him the encouragement that he did not find in his own family.

The three eldest children – Dora, Barbara and Robin – all planned to follow a career in the Arts. Sometimes Ransome and the girls went off in a boat with a picnic tea. At other times they worked indoors. Glimpses of the 20-year old Ransome are to be found in 18-year old Dora Collingwood's journal:

June 3 1904

Last Saturday Mr Ransome came to dinner, he is staying in the village. He has been to dinner every day since. To-day he has been on the water with us from 9 till 7, with an interval for lunch. This evening we stayed in the garden and he tried to make us see fairies. Last night we went on the water after dinner and two other nights we sat down in the wood on the railings till 10. He is coming to stay with us tomorrow.

Naturally, Ransome fell in love with both the girls, but especially with Barbara. Perhaps it was because of his boisterous, high-spirited enthusiasm coupled with a lack of worldliness, that the girls called him 'Toad'. It was to be more than a month before he could drag himself away from the family. Even then Mrs Collingwood had to pack his case because his things were in 'hopeless confusion'. His going left a 'large gap in the household'.

During the next few years he was to see a great deal of the Collingwoods. In 1905 the whole Ransome family spent three weeks at How Head, almost next door. Ransome developed the habit of dropping in on whatever the Collingwoods were doing and staying for hours on end. For their part, the girls found Ransome interesting and unusual. 'He really is a dear in spite of his eccentricities. He is so nice and utterly different from any man I know …' confided Dora, but she recognised that he was self-centred and she also commented on his thoughtlessness. He proposed to both girls more than once, and Barbara took a long time to make up her mind, before refusing him. They remained close friends for the rest of their lives.

No one can be quite sure when Ransome learnt to sail. At Nibthwaite the family only had the use of a rowing boat, and so his first lessons were probably aboard *Swallow* that Barbara and Robin Collingwood sailed on Coniston Water, and which they kept in the boathouse below Lanehead.

For the next four years Ransome's life followed a pattern. The winters were spent in London, hard at work, but each summer he set off for the north. He published some books of essays that are, perhaps, best forgotten. He read widely, and already – so far as his modest income would allow – he had become a book collector. Life in Bohemian London agreed with him. He made a number of friends from among the literati of the time, including the poet Edward Thomas, who shared the same lodgings for a while.

Ransome spent three summers at Wall Nook Farm near Cartmel in order to be near his friend the poet and playwright, Gordon Bottomley. Here he was given a bedroom overlooking the fells and fed very well for his £1 per week. At this time he developed an amazing appetite for his landlady's home-made marmalade.

While he was at Wall Nook he wrote four simple children's nature books: *Pond and Stream*, *The Child's Book of the Seasons*, *Things in our Garden*, *Highways and Byways in Fairyland*. Ransome tried to devote his weekdays to writing and at weekends he walked fifteen miles to see Barbara Collingwood at Lanehead, calling on his way for a pint at the Hark to Melody in Haverthwaite and another at the Red Lion at Lowick Bridge. Often his companion on these walks was the poet Lascelles Abercrombie, who also stayed at Wall Nook. After a day spent on the lake they would walk back to Cartmel in the dark.

In 1908 he stayed at a farm in Low Yewdale, beside the Yewdale Beck. By now he had acquired a tent that in fine weather he would pitch on a mound beside the beck a few yards upstream. In his autobiography he refers to 'a countryside I can call my own' and speaks of otters playing in the moonlight, the heron beside the lake shore and corncrakes in the fields below the bobbin mill. He seems to have been more at home in the valleys than on the high fells. He renewed his

Arthur Ransome beside his tent at Low Yewdale in 1908. The tent 'with ears' was to feature in *Swallows and Amazons* as the tent of the Amazon Pirates. {Author's collection}

boyhood friendship with the charcoal burners in the coppice woodlands and he made new friends from among the Gypsies. Ransome also joined the young men practising Cumberland and Westmorland wrestling for the Grasmere Sports. All this while he continued to haunt the Collingwoods, who always made him welcome.

After Barbara's, and then Dora's refusal of marriage, Ransome seems to have made a habit of proposing to a variety of girls, just for practice. Unfor-

Dora Collingwood, a self portrait

tunately, when he proposed to Ivy Walker in the hot-house atmosphere of artistic London, she ignored her family's advice, broke off her engagement to her cousin, and accepted him. After their marriage in 1909, the couple travelled north to meet Ransome's Lake Country friends. The visit was a failure and three days later they were back in Petersfield, Hampshire, where he and Ivy had set up home. Ivy had thrived in London where she had been the centre of attention, but she was often left alone in the country after her marriage. The following May their daughter Tabitha was born. Later that summer Ransome had a holiday alone, camping in the Lanehead garden and on Peel Island. Ivy, Tabitha and their Jamaican nurse joined them in October and they occupied Lanehead for a couple of months while the Collingwoods were away. Tabitha was christened in Coniston church, but she was never to make a home in the Lake District. For a fortnight in 1912 Dora Collingwood stayed with them in their home in Wiltshire and found it 'a quaint and unusual household'. She liked Ivy and she enjoyed her stay, but she was glad to get away from people who 'live on their emotions to such an extent'.

This was the period of his life when Ransome devoted himself to literary criticism and produced *A History of Story Telling, Edgar Allen Poe*. Of all his literary friends, only John Masefield recognised where Ransome's true gift lay, and urged him to give up literary criticism and write stories. Finally, his book *Oscar Wilde* landed the horrified author in a celebrated court case. The alleged libel was successfully defended and Ivy revelled in the public attention, but the whole worrying experience left Ransome determined never to write anything that could possibly bring him up against the law again. Instead he became interested in folk tales.

Ransome left for Russia in 1913, partly to get away from Ivy, and partly in order to collect Russian fairy

Ransome's first wife Ivy with their daughter Tabitha. (Courtesy Ted Alaxander)

eye-witness reports of the Revolution to the *Daily News* and later to the *Manchester Guardian*. Recently it has been suggested that Ransome might have been a spy for the Cheka, the Russian secret police as well as for the British, and contemporary accounts suggest that his information on British foreign policy was 'very important' to Lenin. Certainly Ransome was well known at the Kremlin, and claimed that he had played chess with Lenin. Recently released documents confirm that he was a British agent. There is no evidence that he actually became involved in spying missions, but he certainly acted as a go-between on more than one occasion. He firmly believed that Russia should be left to sort out her own problems without intervention from the west.

It was while he was gathering bulletins from the Bolsheviks that he met and fell in love with Trotsky's secretary. She was the 'tall, jolly girl', Evgenia Petrovna Shelepina, who was to become his second wife. Evgenia was a high-born young woman whose family lived in a large house next door to an official of the Ministry of Foreign Affairs. She had received a privileged education, and when Ransome was writing the Swallows and Amazons books, she was his harshest critic and his most loyal supporter. One who knew them both at this time was Bruce Lockhart, the Acting Consul-General at Moscow who supported Ransome in his work throughout, and who described him as 'a Don Quixote with a walrus moustache' and Evgenia as 'extremely able and tactful'. No one interested in this eventful period of Ransome's life should miss *Ransome in Russia* by Ted Alexander. Lockhart enabled Evgenia to leave Russia with Ransome by giving her a British passport, and for several years they lived in the Baltic states of Estonia and Latvia while he continued to send reports of the political situation to the *Manchester Guardian*. With his sprig of heather from Peel Island and a lucky stone from the

stories. He loved his little daughter, but he recognised that he could never be happy living with Ivy. He decided that a clean break would be for the best, and he knew that Ivy would be unlikely to follow him to Russia. He appears to have had no difficulty teaching himself the language from children's reading books, and in a couple of years he had collected enough stories to retell to English children in *Old Peter's Russian Tales*, which was published in 1916.

But by then, Ransome had become caught up in the Great War, afterwards remaining in Russia to send

The view across the Winster Valley towards Yorkshire seen from above the Low Ludderburn rooftops.

summit of Coniston Old Man, Ransome seems to have been marking time, until Ivy should agree to a divorce, and he could return to the Lake Country and fishing. Meanwhile, there were compensations for living in Eastern Europe, and after two summers sailing small and unsuitable craft, they had the well-known ketch *Racundra* built for cruising in the Baltic. Their cruise from Riga to Helsingfors and back, with Carl Sehmel as crew, gave Ransome

Racundra's First Cruise, which is still considered one of the finest accounts of small boat cruising. The name *Racundra* has long puzzled people. It is made up of RA (Ransome) C (Carl Sehmel) UND (and) RA (Evgenia). Ransome was still married to Ivy and for delicacy, throughout the book, Evgenia is referred to as The Cook. Sehmel used to recall with amusement that the pipe-smoking cook slept with a pet snake in her bunk. Eventually Ivy agreed to a divorce and

Low Ludderburn, by Roger Wardale after a watercolour by Edith Ransome.

Ransome and Evgenia were married at Reval (now Tallin) in Estonia in May 1924. A year later they settled in the Lake District.

For £550 the Ransomes bought Low Ludderburn, a stone cottage three hundred years old with nearly two acres of land overlooking the Winster valley. The cottage is 400 feet above sea level and about six miles along narrow, winding lanes to the south of Windermere town. Ransome wrote joyfully to his mother:

From the terrace in front of the house you can see Arnside and a strip of sea under the Knott. Away to the left you can see Ingleborough, and from the fell just behind the house you can see Ambleside and all the lake hills. It contains two rooms on the ground floor, plus a scullery hole. Two rooms upstairs. A lean-to in bad repair, capable of being turned into a first-rate kitchen. a huge two-story barn in first-rate condition, stone built, at present with stables below and the top part which has a double door opening on the road is used to put up a Morris Cowley. Water from a Roman well just behind the house, our title deeds giving us the right to lay a pipe from it to the house. A lot of apples, damsons, gooseberries, raspberries, currants, and the whole orchard white with snowdrops and daffodils just coming. Blemishes. Very low beams in the rooms. A good deal to be done to make it really nice. But it is a stout place.

Evgenia was just as enthusiastic. What neither of them mentioned in their letters was that their home was isolated and without electricity or telephone. Life in such a place would have been impossible without a car, and so they acquired what Ransome called 'a perambulating biscuit tin' which 'rattles about beautifully'. The narrow lanes around the cottage require care, and only two days after he had taken over the car, Ransome ran into a wall. Evgenia was the practical one, overseeing the conversion of the upper room of the barn into a wonderfully light and airy workroom with a new wooden floor, a fireplace and a window looking across the valley, at a cost of a further £125. Having seen to this improvement, she began to take the garden in hand.

At that time the *Manchester Guardian* still regarded Ransome as a valuable foreign correspondent, and the paper secured for him a regular income. During the first few years at Ludderburn, he was sent to Egypt, Sudan, Russia and China; visits that he made with increasing reluctance as they settled into their Lakeland home. He was also called upon to contribute leading articles on foreign politics whenever the occasion demanded. It must have been very lonely for Evgenia, living in an isolated cottage in a foreign country during Ransome's months abroad. It is not surprising that she made a point of carefully recording in her diary the time at which the postman called each day! Shopping in Windermere involved a hilly round trip of twelve miles and it was just as well that Evgenia quickly became accustomed to walking uphill.

They both delighted in the wildlife that surrounded their home and enjoyed watching the nesting redstarts and spotted flycatchers. Both their diaries have records of sightings of goldcrests, long-tailed tits and red squirrels. Ransome obtained permission to fish the upper reaches of the River Winster before they had moved in, and he found that he had only to go through the orchard and down the footpath for half a mile or so in order to reach the best stretch of water. He was soon writing happily to his mother that he had caught eight trout in an afternoon. Fishing was a pastime that Evgenia could share, and she often accompanied him on trips on the lake and to the nearby rivers. Among their friends, she gained a reputation for making the most delicious fish soup from perch. They bought a rowing boat when they first moved to Ludderburn, and from 1929 they were able sail *Swallow* to the head of Windermere for tea at the Wateredge Hotel in about an hour. Favourite picnic spots were the island of Blake Holme and one of the Lilies of the Valley islands behind Belle Isle. They entered *Swallow* in 'all-comers' races and would return from a sail very wet, but having thoroughly enjoyed the little craft battling with the wind and water.

Charles Renold from Cheadle in Cheshire was a fisherman with whom Ransome formed a close friendship. His wife, Margaret did not share her husband's passion for fishing but she was an avid reader, and Ransome quickly came to value her ideas when a plot would not go right for him. Other regular visitors to Ludderburn were Ted Scott, son of the editor of the *Manchester Guardian,* and his son Dick, who were duly introduced to the pleasures of Windermere.

Ransome began a regular fishing column for the *Manchester Guardian* as soon as he was settled in at Low Ludderburn, and this gave him an excuse to fish over a wider area. He fished the Cumberland Derwent, the Hodder, the Ribble, the Eden and the Dove. He also commented on country matters and these articles show him to be an environmentalist ahead of his time. More than once he used his column to contribute an attack on the speeding motor-boats on Windermere:

Towards the end of April motor boats appear, and now, when the fishing should be really worthwhile, these monstrous creatures with a crew of one or perhaps two are roaring up and down the lake, creating a vibration that can be felt from one side of the lake to the other and making the surface of the lake a patchwork quilt (there is no other way of describing the effect of the oil they exude).

He also spoke out strongly against the practice of tarring country roads:

Not far from where I am writing there is a delightful little beck flowing out into Morecambe Bay, full of decent little trout and frequented by salmon in the spawning season. A few days ago, thanks to the road authorities, there was so much tar on the roads that the rains blackened the stream, in the words of the local postman who actually saw the dead fish floating down it. If this sort of thing is to go on unchecked it will not be long before our trout and salmon rods will be treasured in museums as 'instruments used in the early twentieth century in the capture of now extinct aquatic creatures.'

'Exercise' by Evgenia Ransome.

'Rest' by Evgenia Ransome.

These were unusual outbursts: more typical is this example of Ransome's ability to express his love of the lake country:

> So far, everywhere on the rivers, the main pleasure of fishing has been that of being at the waterside, where, after all, there is much to be seen besides fish. This is the season when a man may see a cloud of long-tailed tits blowing through the leafless bushes that overhang the river. Wrens are busy and show the fisherman where they are and what they are about by going into shrill hysterics and scolding him as if they were prepared to drive him out of the river. Dippers are building. Herons, of course, are about as usual, but I have not seen a kingfisher this year.

Fifty of the best of these fishing pieces were brought together in book form and published in 1929 under the title of *Rod and Line*. This delightful collection is considered to be one of the most important books on fishing, and it was followed more than sixty years later with another collection, *Arthur Ransome on Fishing*, in which Jeremy Swift, himself a fisherman, also contributes a long introduction to Ransome's fishing life.

Often, Ransome's spasmodic diary entries were records of the arrival of the swallows, the first blooming of the daffodils or the catching of eight trout in the River Crake. However he was not above taking his gun to any rabbit or pheasant unwise enough to stray on to his land. At New Year 1928 he and Evgenia, climbed through the snow to the top of Ludderburn Hill so that they could hear the sound of church bells from across the valley. It became an annual celebration, though life at Ludderburn was not entirely idyllic. Evgenia fought a constant battle against marauding sheep that had developed a fancy for her flowers, and on one occasion a plague of field mice threatened to overrun the cottage. Their cat Winkle

Evgenia with a large pike, Low Ludderburn (Photo: Arthur Ransome, courtesy Abbot Hall)

gave birth to three silver-grey kittens that they took to The Cat Show at Crystal Palace, where the trio were Highly Commended. Two of the kittens, Polly and Podge, they kept.

The workroom was Ransome's special pride. The large worktable was covered by a grey blanket and littered with all sorts of keepsakes, as well as his writing things and the typewriter. There were big shelves teeming with books, files and rows of diaries, and around the large room were comfortable chairs, whilst looking down from high on a wall was a stuffed fish. It was in this workroom that he wrote *Swallows and Amazons*, carrying the manuscript up to his bedroom at night so as to be able to lean out and touch it from his bed. Once he had a bad fall while going down the steep hill at Birks Brow, 'listening to Dorothea', and had to crawl more than half a mile home with a broken ankle. For some time after the accident he was unable to indulge in his habit of pacing up and down the workroom while he thought.

The Ludderburn years were the most creative of Ransome's life, but there was a price to pay. He had developed a duodenal ulcer, brought on by worrying over money. Thereafter, he never went anywhere without his small leather attaché case containing bottles of bismuth, wholemeal biscuits and some milk, taken at regular intervals. Publisher's deadlines and bouts of depression, which seem to have overtaken him at some stage in the preparation of every book, only served to make matters worse. He sought help in Harley Street and tried a variety of cures without a great deal of success until he was ordered to put on weight, give up journalism for good and never use aluminium cooking pots again.

There were still plenty of interesting diversions to take his mind off the worry of the moment. In 1933, when Charles and Margaret Renold became interested in sailing, they camped on one of the Windermere islands and were taken sailing in *Swallow*. The following winter they had own boat built by the Arnside boatbuilder who had built *Swallow*, and Ransome enthusiastically supervised the building. The little boat was given the name *Coch-y-bonddhu* after a fishing fly, but from the first it was always called *Cocky*. Ransome noted in his diary that when *Cocky* raced *Swallow* she beat her by the length of Belle Isle. Later that summer Ransome raced *Cocky* again: 'Genia was cold and found *Cocky* too small and generally did not enjoy herself. It was a pity we tried it. But the little boat sailed jolly well. One of the big ones was dismasted.' Charles Renold found that he preferred fishing to small boat sailing, and somehow *Cocky* became Ransome's. His internal problems always seemed to clear up when he was sailing, and although *Racundra* had been sold in order to buy the cottage, they had never given up the hope of being able to continue the sort of cruising that had come to an end when they returned to England.

By the summer of 1935 the Swallows books were selling well, and Ransome was able to buy a 7-ton cutter and rename it *Nancy Blackett*. Ludderburn and *Swallow* were sold and they rented a house close to the River Orwell in Suffolk. He managed to spend a good deal of time afloat during the next four summers and once made a notable North Sea crossing to Holland in order to be sure of the details of the unsought voyage in *We Didn't Mean to Go to Sea*. With the outbreak of the Second World War he became land-bound again, and a letter from Barbara Collingwood, now married and settled near Coniston and full of Lake District news, made him think longingly of the lakes once more. He said in a letter to his mother in August 1940:

> ... the area is full of holiday-makers asking the way, as all sign posts have been removed, even the little board on the Hawkshead road that said 'To the Tarns'. I must

Arthur Ransome at around the age of twenty by Dora Collingwood.
(Courtesy Taqui Altounyan)

say it all made me very homesick for a look at the lakes and a run or rather crawl up to the top of the Old Man, but I can't possibly stir from here in the present circuses *(sic)*.

The circumstances changed more quickly than he could have foreseen. Evgenia suffered much more from the air-raids and disturbed nights than her husband, and when they learned that they could be turned out of their home at twenty-four-hours notice, she agreed to return to the Lake District. A couple of months later Ransome wrote a very different letter to his mother:

… being back in the lakes makes everything look pretty good. You know I had quite made up my mind that nothing would get Genia to come back. I don't think anything would except the war, which of course got lively in our parts very early on … now she is back, she seems very pleased … though the rooms are so tiny that we can't move without hitting our funny-bones. There is none of that shut-in feeling she didn't like at Lanehead, and the house itself has none of the primitive savagery of Ludderburn. First-rate water supply for one thing.

Their new home was The Heald, situated mid-way along the road that runs down the east side of Coniston Water and surrounded by pine trees. With the bungalow went seventeen acres of lovely woodland and half a mile of lake frontage. Close at hand was a wooden jetty where they moored *Coch-y-bonddhu*.

The Ransomes were optimistic when they set out with Polly and Podge on their journey, and for a while Evgenia felt better, but the reality proved disappointing. For one thing, The Heald was even more isolated than Ludderburn. The nearest shop was in Coniston village five miles around the head of the lake and the weekly shopping expedition to Ulverston involved a trip of 18 miles. Petrol rationing meant that after they had fuelled the electricity generator they had next to no petrol left. Ransome took to a light motor-bike ('The Monster'), but Evgenia was not so fortunate. The damp weather did not agree with her and the poor soil frustrated her gardening ambitions. Instead, she kept chickens.

It was not long before Ransome suffered two ruptures and his doctor told him that his sailing and fell-walking days were over. He could, however, fish *quietly*. For some time he was unable to row his boat, so he painstakingly learnt to fish for Coniston char under sail, as he explained to his mother:

Last night we had a most luxurious supper on a brace of char, each close to half a pound (big for Coniston) caught by sailing. The trouble comes when you hook your fish sixty to eighty yards way and have to manage sail, rudder, rod, reel and net at one and the same time with only two hands and false teeth. But the thing can be done and last night's supper was the proof of it.

The Ransomes had a hard time at The Heald, and by 1945 they were trying unsuccessfully to take up their old life on the East Coast. They could not find suitable property in the area in which they wanted to live and settled in London. Ransome commissioned a new boat, which he called a 'marine bath-chair' and to which the designer gave the name *Peter Duck*. 'It will be plain *PD*,' grumbled Ransome. They never took to the boat, although it has proved a highly successful design and 38 were built.

After one frustrating summer with the boat, they bought Lowick Hall, only five miles across the valley from the scene of his childhood holidays. Not only did they take on the hall but also the adjacent farm as well and 130 acres. The whole enterprise was financially and physically too much for them. The roof leaked, some of the floors were rotten and the place needed new drainage. After a couple of months Ransome was 'very disheartened' and a year later Evgenia had had enough: 'Genia says she wants to give up Lowick. Impossible with no staff.' Evgenia had never been able to get on with servants. Ransome, however, quickly managed to slip back into his old ways, fishing, sailing *Cocky* on Windermere, playing cards and chess with friends and taking pot-shots at any stoat invading his lawn. But the Lake District was changing. On one occasion while sailing on Windermere, he landed on Blake Holme only to be disturbed by the sound of a radio blaring from the nearby shore. Even at Lowick Hall his peace could be interrupted: 'Large well-dressed girl in garden with two others. When told she really ought not to be in someone else's garden she shouted

Arthur Ransome aged around 25. (Author's collection)

23

out that I was a blackguard and a parasite!!!'

They parted with Lowick Hall in 1950, after two years of pouring money into the place, and took a flat in Putney overlooking the Thames. They managed to continue cruising on the South Coast and across the Channel until 1954 when Ransome finally accepted that his sailing days were over. From 1955 until they finally relinquished their London flat in 1963, they spent the summers in the Lake District and the winters in town. At first they rented Ealinghearth Cottage at Haverthwaite, and then nearby Hill Top that eventually they bought. Ransome managed to continue fishing until 1960, but a fall in 1958 began a long, sad decline. Ever optimistic, he tried to drive a Morris Minor car as late as 1961, when he was 77. When the attempt failed, he was effectively a prisoner at Hill Top except when friends were able to take him for a drive. Hill Top was yet another remote cottage and quite unsuitable for anyone's final years. Yet he was still able to find pleasure in natural history and a present of a jar of tadpoles and a grass snake brought him 'great delight'.

In 1962 he allowed the BBC to make a filmed serial of *Swallows and Amazons* and, having done so, immediately regretted it, as he told his old sailing friend Colonel Busk:

> … horrid children with loathsome voices and so forth . . . and where will they find the brats to be filmed while sailing? And where will they find S and A, the two boats? They have already plumped for the wrong island (with no harbour). In fact general prospect of horror.

The surviving copy of the film with Titty in a duffel coat and the children wearing life-jackets, seems to support his view, although they did use the proper houseboat, which the otherwise splendid 1974 film failed to do.

As Ransome became more frail, he grew increasingly dependent on Evgenia who struggled on with her sciatica for as long as she could. In October 1965, after her second heart attack and Ransome's second stroke, she transferred him to Cheadle Royal Hospital in Manchester where he died eighteen months later. One of his regular visitors during that time was Dick Kelsall. Ransome was desperately ill but his eyes lit up whenever Kelsall spoke of the days when they had all lived in the Winster Valley.

Chapter Two

The Coming of the Swallows

Anyone looking for the origin of *Swallows and Amazons* will be confronted by Ransome's note, written in 1958, which has appeared in all subsequent editions:

> I have been often asked how I came to write *Swallows and Amazons*. The answer is that it had its beginning long, long ago when, as children my brother, my sisters and I spent most of our holidays on a farm at the south end of Coniston. We played in or on the lake or on the hills about it finding friends in the farmers and shepherds and charcoal-burners whose smoke rose from the coppice woods along the shore. We adored the place. Coming to it we used to run down to the lake, dip our hands in and wish, as if we had just seen the new moon. Going away from it we were half-drowned in tears. While away from it, as children and as grown ups, we dreamt about it. No matter where I was, wandering about the world, I used at night to look for the North Star and in my mind's eye, could see the beloved skyline of great hills beneath it. *Swallows and Amazons* grew out of those memories. I could not help writing it. It almost wrote itself.

One of Ransome's earliest published efforts was a series of whimsical little nature books for children. In the third of these, *Pond and Stream* (1906), the Imp and the Elf, having looked at a beck and met a dipper, are drawn towards 'a little rocky island' on the lake. The book was written shortly after Ransome had become a member of the Collingwood family circle and there is a clear reference to Collingwood's Norse saga *Thorstein of the Mere*.

> We ran the boat carefully aground in a pebbly inlet at one end of the island. We take the baskets ashore, and camp in the shadow of a little group of pines ... As soon as the tea is over we prowl over the rockiness of the little island, and creep among the hazels and pines and tiny oaks and undergrowth ... When we have picked our way through to the other end, we climb upon a high rock with a flat top to it, and heather growing in its crevices, and here we lie, torpid after our tea, and pretend we are Viking folk from the north who have forced our way here by land and sea, and are looking for the first time upon a lake that no one knew before us.

Swallows and Amazons evidently grew out of *Pond and Stream*, for even in this apprentice work there is an almost poetic response to the Lake District. In crossing between reality and imagination, Ransome makes use of a device which was to become one of the strongest features of *Swallows and Amazons*: '*Swallow* and her crew moved steadily southward over a desolate ocean sailed for the first time by white seamen.'

Ransome's carefully prepared note, however, tells only part of the story. After *Pond and Stream*, twenty-two years were to pass before some children that he knew slightly, came to his childhood playground at Coniston, and their visit gave him the impetus to write *Swallows and Amazons*. These were the children of Dora Collingwood and the Irish-Armenian surgeon Ernest Altounyan, sometimes seen as a rival to Ransome in the affection of the Collingwood sisters. In fact, Dora did not meet Altounyan until after Ransome's first marriage.

For some years they had been living in Syria where Altounyan helped his father to run the well-known hospital at Aleppo. The family returned to Coniston for a long stay at the home of Dora's parents at Lanehead, arriving at the end of April 1928, complete with the family – Taqui (Barbara) aged 11, Susie (9), Titty (Mavis) aged 8, Roger (6), Bushie (Brigit) aged 2 and their Armenian nurse.

Ernest Altounyan was a sailing enthusiast, and had decided his four eldest children were ready to learn to sail. They stayed at Bank Ground, the farm just below their grandparent's home at Lanehead, as the elderly couple were unable to cope with eight visitors for a long stay. Hardly had they established themselves at Bank Ground when Altounyan went off to Barrow in Furness and bought two sturdy dinghies for £15 apiece. The story goes that Ransome and Altounyan came to an agreement that, when the Altounyans returned to Syria, one of the little boats would become Ransome's and he would pay his share.

From time to time the Ransomes drove over to Coniston and fished for perch, while the children sailed in circles by the Lanehead boathouse. Altounyan saw to it that the children behaved in a proper seamanlike manner. In those days, even harmlessly trailing a hand in the water was frowned upon as the behaviour of a tripper. Both Ransome and Altounyan believed that, so far as possible, people should be allowed to discover how to do things for themselves. Taqui and Titty sailed in *Mavis*, a narrow white-painted dinghy with a white standing lug sail and a heavy iron centreplate, that would have been far too much for 11-year old Taqui to lift unaided. *Mavis* is 13 feet long and had been built at Piel Island near Barrow. Taqui always remembered the thrill of jumping aboard *Mavis* and feeling the boat come alive beneath her feet. The other children thought her 'rather a tub'. They all preferred *Swallow*, the more attractive dinghy they named after the old Coniston *Swallow* sailed by their parents. *Swallow* was the same length and was also white, but it had a brown top strake and a brown sail. It was a much roomier boat and had no centre-board for Susie and Roger to struggle with. *Swallow* was built by Crossfields of Arnside shortly before World War One. Susie remembered how Uncle Arthur showed them how to fish in the shallow water by the lake shore. Titty loved those windless days spent fishing over the transom with her legs dangling above the water. Roger used to have the job of keeping *Mavis* bailed out, but he preferred splashing around in the tiny dinghy they called *Toob* or *Tub*.

The Altounyan children remained at Bank Ground Farm until the following January, and when it was no longer possible to sail, generously agreed that they would keep *Mavis*, so that Ransome could have *Swallow*, and the little boat was shipped to Bowness and stored for the winter. Shortly before they were due to leave, it was Ransome's birthday, and the following afternoon there were cries of 'Many happy returns,' as Taqui and Titty appeared at Low Ludderburn holding a splendid pair of red leather slippers which they had bought in an Aleppo souk as a present. Their father hid behind the garden wall awaiting developments, for Ransome had told him that he was busy and that if he should come to Low Ludderburn at all, he should leave the children behind. Ransome stormed down from his workroom in the barn, but his heavy frown soon melted away and Altounyan felt it safe to come out of hiding. Ransome was touched by the children's gift and by their generosity in allowing him to have *Swallow,* and there was a sad parting at Windermere station a couple of days later.

After their departure, Ransome began to think what fun they would all have if he could write a book for the Altounyans. He could even use some of their names. Ransome was careful to omit details of physical characteristics. We are never told if the Swallows are tall or short, dark or fair-haired, although when Webb and Ransome came to draw the Swallows they are shown with dark hair. The children in Spurrier's illustrations had plenty of naturally curly hair and this would have conflicted with Ransome's view that his

Young Altounyans. Susie, Taqui and Roger, with Titty seated. (Author's collection)

readers would identify with his characters more easily if he was not precise about appearances. The reference to Nancy and Peggy's curly hair showing round their red woollen knitted caps was cut from the early draft. Similarly, he thought that a good spread of ages, hinted at, but not specified, would aid readers, as they became older.

Among Ransome's notes is a sheet written at the conclusion of the series that lets out some of the secrets:

Chronology

Swallows and Amazons	Summer 1930
Roger 7, Titty 9, Susan 11, Peggy 11, John 12, Nancy 12.	
Swallowdale	1931
Winter Holiday	1931-2
Coot Club	Easter 1932
Pigeon Post	Summer hols 1932. First 2 weeks
We Didn't Mean to Go to Sea	Summer hols 1932. Fourth week
Secret Water	Summer hols 1932. End
The Big Si	Summer hols 1932. End September
The Picts and the Martyrs	First fortnight of summer hols 1933
R 10, T 12. S 14, J 15, D [Dorothea] 13, D 12, N 15, P 14, Pete 10, Bill 11, Joe 12	
Second fortnight Swallows and Co [Coots in the North]	

Sharp-eyed readers will have noticed that the events of *Swallowdale* are supposed to have taken place the year after *Swallows and Amazons*, yet the treaty of offence and defence is dated 1929 and the successful expedition to the summit of Kanchenjunga is 1931. With this private note, Ransome corrected the error, although *Swallows and Amazons* has never been changed.

There is another family of children that is frequently overlooked by seekers after the origin of the Walkers – Ransome's own. Arthur was the oldest of the family and his sister, Cecily was a year or so younger. John and Susan perhaps? Next came Geoffrey, three years Arthur's junior, and finally Joyce who was eight years younger. There is certainly some resemblance to the shape of the Walker family. When faced with creating his children, was Ransome's creative process similar to that of J.M. Barrie, who said that he had not focussed on the char-

acteristics of any one boy, but rather that Peter Pan was concocted by rubbing the five Davies boys together, or were each of his characters based on a single person? John Walker, the eldest of the Swallows, was a steady, capable boy of whom Ransome's father would have approved. Throughout the series John's actions are shaped by a sense of duty and the standards he has been set by his father, a naval officer, and it is clear from the start that he intends to follow his father into the Royal Navy. Although he is protective of the younger members of the family, he is content to let Susan minister to their needs and happy to defer to Titty's romantic imagination. It is not clear where the name came from. Perhaps it was coincidence that John Walker was a well-known Bowness boatmen whose name was still to be seen over the door of one of the boat hirer's huts in the 1960s. The early notes for *Swallows and Amazons* were made in a Walker's loose-leaf binder. Walker was also the maiden name of his first wife.

Susan Walker took Susie Altounyan's name, but several of those who remember Genia, including Susie herself, saw more than a passing resemblance to Ransome's own whistle-blowing mate and cook. Mate Susan is probably the least popular of the main characters and her acceptance of maternal and domestic responsibilities makes her almost unique in children's literature. Even Captain John accepts that he must fall in with her housekeeping arrangements. Captain Flint heaps praise upon her, and it is she who enables the Swallows to escape from parental care. She is also the focus for the Walkers as a family unit.

Able-seaman Titty Walker has some of Titty Altounyan's characteristics and of course her 'rather silly' nickname. Possibly she was rubbed against Ransome's sister Joyce who wrote children's books in later life. The resulting spark was a bright one, for Titty Walker is one of Ransome's most original and best-loved characters. Among his papers is a note explaining the name: 'Titty is short for Tittymouse and Tittymouse is long for – it may be Ann or it may be Jane. I do not know; but as she is never known by any other name, it does not seem to matter. She was a very good Able Seaman.' Titty is an ardent reader and a dreamer whose imagination bridges fantasy and reality. As Ernest Altounyan was quick to recognise, Titty is the real hero of *Swallows and Amazons*.

The Boy Roger is likely to have been a similar mix of Roger Altounyan and Ransome's younger brother Geoffrey. For the most part Roger is content to follow John and Titty, but he has a lively sense of fun and an independent streak, and refuses to accept the family view that motor boats are only 'engines in tin boxes'.

Ransome freely accepted that without the Altounyan children he would not have created the Swallows, as he mentioned in a letter to his mother during his visit to Syria in 1932:

> … I must say it seems a little queer now after living with them all in *S & A* and *Swallowdale*, to meet them once more as actual human beings running about. My lot seem to me the solider, but Ernest's are very nice, and eager to know 'What is going to happen to us next?'

What of the Amazons? Ransome said that they sprung from a glimpse of two girls playing by the shore of the lake, one day whilst he was sailing on Coniston. Most of Ransome's sailing on Coniston took place before the First World War when he used to borrow *Jamrach*, or the first *Swallow*, from the Lanehead boathouse. Barbara and Dora Collingwood were not at all like the Amazons, but the idea of sisters who did everything together, might have sprung from them. Their mother (Edith Mary) was known in later life as Molly. In *Swallowdale*, Ransome called the mother of the Amazons Molly. Was this just a coincidence?

Whoever they were, the more intriguing puzzle is to try to discover if Captain Nancy Blackett, Terror of the Seas had an original? There has been more speculation about Nancy's creation than that of any of the other characters. It is here that the resemblance to Barrie's Peter Pan is strongest, for Nancy seems to be a combination of several strong-willed, imaginative girls that Ransome had known, including Taqui Altounyan, whose letters to Ransome are very reminiscent of Nancy. W.G. Collingwood implied that Ruth-Nancy was his granddaughter Ruth, Robin

Titty Altounyan Titty was the Ransomes' favourite, and the childless Ransomes would have liked to adopt her. Instead, they were given this portrait painted by her mother. (Courtesy Taqui Altounyan)

Collingwood's child. She might seem a little young, having been born in 1921, but Ransome was having a huge game with people and their names, as well as the locations, and we can only speculate.

Ransome's biographer, Hugh Brogan, saw a resemblance between Ransome's boyhood friend Ric Eddison and Nancy. Alternatively, Pauline Marshall, in her childhood memoir *How it all Began,* puts the case for herself and her elder sister Georgie being the original girls. They spent their holidays at Bank Ground and as a couple of spirited and adventurous tomboys they could have been the girls that Ransome had seen playing by the shore. Pauline recalls that following her first meeting with Ransome some time after publication of *Swallows and Amazons,* her father told her that they were the Amazons. The boisterous Nancy, setting the tune for everybody, is Ransome's most memorable creation. Her reputation for wildness is well-deserved, but from time to time there are glimpses of someone who is fiercely loyal to her family and friends and supportive of the younger ones, notably Titty and Dick. Peggy is simply the younger sister who is given to chattering in the early novels and is afraid of thunder, and whose very ordinariness makes her the ideal foil for Nancy.

Ransome wrote *Swallows and Amazons* for the Altounyans, to comfort them in what he saw as their exile in the desert, in return for the slippers. This is quite clear in the dedication:

TO
THE SIX FOR WHOM IT WAS WRITTEN
IN EXCHANGE FOR
A PAIR OF SLIPPERS

Originally, Ransome had settled on the number four, but must have changed his mind in order to include their parents. Brigit was still only three, and as he said in his notes, did not count. It was intended to be a very personal gift in which the Altounyans could share his fun. Ransome hoped his friends would delight in the references and jokes that only insiders like themselves could understand. Nobody could have foreseen that the book would become famous and that it would be followed by eleven further stories that would bring sales of five million copies in the U.K. alone. Evgenia withdrew the dedication from *Swallows and Amazons* after her husband's death in 1967 and it has only recently been replaced. When he wrote *Swallows and Amazons,* Ransome could have had no idea that he was writing a best-seller, or that he would be besieged by questioners asking, 'Are they real?' Nobody foresaw that the game would rebound on both Altounyans and the author, or that its origin would come under such scrutiny.

The Altounyans were delighted with their present and Dora immediately wrote to say they all liked it *enormously.* Ransome was immensely gratified. But when Ernest Altounyan's response showed that he identified too closely with the Walkers, Ransome became very depressed. In a letter beginning 'Dear Captain Flint', Altounyan wrote: 'What I most especially like and marvel at is your extraordinary accurate characterisation of the kids. Each is just right – as far as I know them … You've made me to bulge with paternal pride, and I kept saying to myself as I read, damn fine sporting kids and then realising that they were mine … Captain Flint is a very good *you* … I am personally quite content to go down to posterity as the author of the famous Duffer telegram. Dora is a little plaintive about her knowledge of kangaroos and what Bushie will say when she finds out that she has been libelled as Vicky I shudder to think'

This was going too far. Altounyan believed Taqui was Captain John, and for a while, that is how she signed her letters to Ransome. He was also wrong about Mrs Walker, whose Australian background was borrowed from Ransome's own family. The children, however, understood that the book was really written for and not about them, but they all joined in Ransome's game, and Titty in particular seems to have tried to become like the able seaman so as to please Uncle Arthur. No matter who provided the starting point, all the characters owed more to Ransome's creative genius than they did to any living people.

Yet ever after that happy start, Ransome's gift has proved to be a mixed blessing. The characters seemed so real that readers who knew of the Altounyan involvement expected to find them like their fictional selves. When Taqui came to school in England she had to explain that she was not Captain John, and when the balletomane Susie Altounyan went to stay with school friends, she had to live down the 'Mate Susan' tag. Her hosts were quite relieved to find that, although she had lit fires and boiled kettles on Peel Island, she was not like Susan at all! As Taqui has said, 'We must have been pretty nearly the only children in England who did not spend our time playing Swallows and Amazons.'

Ransome's draft, 'How Swallows and Amazons Came to be Written' continues:

The book went on and on and grew bigger and bigger and instead of getting tired of it, I should have liked to be doing nothing else. I was enjoying my own childhood over again, all the best bits of it and the bits that might have been ever so much better if only something or other had been different. But then, as the book did at last come to an end (though there was no reason why I should have gone on for ever) I began to be very much afraid. For though the children in the book had taken things so much into their own hands that I could never be quite sure what they were going to do next, there they were, labelled with the names of the Walkers. And, oddly enough, I could not change their names, though

it sounds so simple, just to go through the book with a pen and put new names in and cross out the old ones. As soon as I tried to change a name, there was a sort of revolt among the people in the book and nothing would go right. So there could be no possible pretending that the people in the book were not the people they actually were. There is a clause about libel between authors and publishers, and when I looked it up I did not like the look of it. Besides that, the Walkers were among my best friends, and I began to wonder what would have happened if they did not like their portraits, and still worse, if Captain John and Mate Susan and Able seaman Titty and the Boy Roger did not like theirs. And yet, I thought, even if the people outside the book don't like the people inside the book, the people inside have got some sort of right to be alive.'

He goes on to describe how 'Mr Walker' and his 'enormous family' came to the lake and sailed 'a regular fleet' of small boats including *Swallow* (there is no mention of *Mavis*). Ransome has clearly embroidered the truth a little.

Old friends sometimes quarrel and when, near the end of their lives Ransome and Altounyan had become irreconcilable, Ransome tried to suppress the Altounyan children's part in his story. Altounyan had made too many claims on behalf of his family and implied that Ransome had simply taken his children as models, or perhaps Ransome was unconsciously jealous of a man who had succeeded in marrying a Collingwood. Almost thirty years later, in a part of his autobiography that was edited out of the published version after his death by Sir Rupert Hart-Davies, he wrote very differently:

The children concerned are grown up now, some of them with children of their own, so that no feelings will be hurt if I tell the story of the mess into which I dived as a result of my benevolent but idiotic impulses. *Swallows and Amazons* was already sketched out and the characters already named and living their own lives when, one day when I was working very hard, a car pulled up at Ludderburn and I saw Ernest Altounyan step out. I had already warned him that I was overwhelmed with work and for some days would have no time for visitors. I was very cross at seeing him and was moving towards the gate (wishing to forestall any invasion of the barn where all the tables were covered with sheets of my book) when it opened and two of the Altounyan children came through each holding out a red leather Arab slipper. My crossness ebbed away in a backwash of shame. I thought of those little Easterners going back to Aleppo and Syria, while the little English children of my book would be sailing in *Swallow* which I had allowed to remain on Coniston for a summer so that the little Altounyans should have two boats to play with. It occurred to me that it would be fun for the little Altounyans if I altered the names in my book so that they could at least pretend that the adventures in it were their own. It was not possible to take all their names, but I took three, Susan, Titty and Roger. My eldest was a boy, John, and I could not change him into a girl to match the eldest Altounyan, who was a girl called Taqui. But I did what I could, and, when the book was published and they read the dedication and remembered the incident of the slippers, they adopted my characters as their own and the generous-hearted Taqui said she did not at all mind being John. I had been a little afraid that their parents would object, but on the contrary, the time was to come when I had to answer an enquiry from Cambridge as to whether it was really true that Ernest Altounyan had sent the original of the telegram 'Better drowned than duffers if not duffers will not drown'. The whole family accepted responsibility for being the characters in my tale, though Dora did say that she did not understand why I had to give her an Australian grandmother.

The joke once started had to be kept up. I used to write to the Altounyans about 'our' children, and as for the children themselves it was clear that I must never, while they were children, deprive them of the 'selves' they had so willingly adopted. This was all very well while they were in Syria, but was more than awkward in later years when it became difficult to reconcile, in the minds of people who knew both, these children of Aleppo, much of whose charm depended on their Eastern-ness with my four children who were just about as English as they could be. At first there was no difficulty for me because when I was writing *Swallows and Amazons*, I had hardly seen the Altounyan children half a dozen times and so had not been able to do more than borrow three of their names. It became more and more difficult when I had to deal with hordes of letters from other children asking 'Are they real?' and begging for their addresses, and with such letters as that of an American lady who wrote inviting me to bring (at her expense) the whole party of Swallows and Amazons over to America to spend the summer with her and her son. I had to find a formula that would not make my children less real for others than they were for me. I found one that served ...' The only way to keep a secret (your own and other people's) is NEVER to answer a question.' I do not know yet what is the proper attitude in the presence of such questioners. My children were much more real to me than most of the people I knew. I had spent so much time with them. I knew so much more about them then ever I could put down on paper. It was a painful shock to be forced to remember that there are more kinds of reality than one. And it was made much worse when children wrote almost with indignation that they had met people who had told them that they were the Swallows and that they were not at all like the children in my books. I lamented many times that I had ever yielded to impulse and started or even helped the misunderstanding on its way.

No matter. Though the Altounyan children remarked, 'if you are writing about us, hadn't you better come and see us to find out what we are like?' they grew up in time, while all the adventures of my English family happened between 1929 and 1933, and with the increasing disparity in age the difficulty lessened, though I never got over the slight discomfort, when I met the little Easterners even when grown up and married, and always felt I had to protect *my* children against these very different people moving in a different world.

This version is not supported by Ransome's working notes in which Susan, Titty and Roger are the only names which remain unchanged, nor does it square with the entries in his diary. Nevertheless, it is hard not to sympathise with Ransome's difficulty in answering children's questions. Perhaps his reluctance to face their enquiries gave rise to his reputation for disliking children.

In *Swallows and Amazons* the Walker family stay at Holly Howe, a farm which was recognisable from the text as High Bank Ground Farm below Lanehead, even before Clifford Webb's drawing appeared in the second edition, and which Dora thought 'has quite a look of Bank Ground though wrong in almost every detail'. In the drafts for the story Ransome actually uses the name Bank Ground and only at the last minute did he change the name to Holly Howe. The name comes from a large house to the north of Coniston village that today serves as a Youth Hostel. Holly Howe, like Bank Ground, lies above a field sloping down to some boathouses beside a lake. The lake is essentially Windermere, with additions from Coniston Water, and while many places are easily recognised, others have some degree of literary camouflage. Years later, Ransome confided to Lady Liddell-Hart that one shore of his lake was Coniston

Holly Howe. *Roger, aged seven, and no longer the youngest of the family, ran in wide zigzags, to and fro, across the steep field that sloped up to Holly Howe, the farm where they were staying for part of the summer holidays.* **Swallows and Amazons**

and the other was Windermere, but it is more complicated than this.

While the children are waiting for permission from their absent father to borrow the sailing dinghy *Swallow* and camp on a nearby island, they look out from the Peak in Darien just as, some years before, Ransome had looked out from the rock at Reval (now Tallin) across the Baltic to the island of Nargon. The peak in Darien has been variously identified, but it extends as the left-hand promontory of a very deep bay in which there is a boathouse. Just such a bay can be found at the head of Windermere and at its mouth is the little cliff known as Gale Naze Crag. When their father's telegram arrives giving permission, the Walkers (now the Swallows) set sail across uncharted waters. The lake has no ferry, but otherwise the life of Windermere, with its fishermen, steamers and racing yachts, is faithfully portrayed as a background to the children's imaginative play. The other lake users are regarded by the children as mere 'natives'.

On their voyage of discovery the Swallows are intrigued by the sight of a fat man living on a houseboat. At that time the *Esperance,* was moored in the bay south of Cockshot point on Windermere and used by Sir Samuel Scott's family as a houseboat. Stephen Spurrier's lively map decorated the end papers of *Swallows and Amazons* for many years, but his illustrations were heartily disliked by Ransome and never used. They do, however, confirm the identification by closely resembling photographs taken at the time. Some years later Ransome admitted the connection, when he confessed to Sir Samuel's son, that he had once pulled alongside the houseboat and peeped through the windows!

Wild Cat Island with its steep, rocky

Darien *The children had found their way to the trees through the far end of the promontory where it dropped, like a cliff, into the lake.* **Swallows and Amazons**

sides and harbour is mostly Peel Island. W.G. Collingwood gave away this secret as long ago as 1932 in *The Lake Counties*. Anyone who has taken a boat into the hidden harbour on Peel Island, splashed ashore and scrambled over the rocks, needs little convincing that they have landed on Wild Cat Island. However, Ransome cooked up another juicy red herring by declaring in a letter that the island was Blake Holm on Windermere; an assertion perpetuated by Evgenia. Although *Swallows and Amazons* needed the impetus of the Altounyans, it is firmly rooted in Ransome's childhood holidays of a hundred years ago – and Peel Island was central to these memories.

Having spent their first night on the island, the explorers collect their milk from a conveniently situated nearby farm, just as Evgenia explained. Christina Hardyment in her jolly account of exploration and discovery, *Arthur Ransome and Captain Flint's Trunk* revealed how she had found a sketch-plan Ransome made of Dixon's Farm. From this she deduced it

was based on Low Yewdale Farm, where Ransome had stayed as a young man, so as to be near the Collingwoods.

The Swallows spend the first few days fishing and gently settling down to life on the island. Everything changes after the Amazons sail round the island flying the skull and crossbones. Soon the Swallows and Amazons have become allies and have embarked upon a 'war'. The Amazons live at Beckfoot, a large, grey-stone house with a lawn leading down to a river shortly before it enters the lake. At the edge of the

Holly Howe Boathouse. *The boathouse was a stone one, with a narrow quay along each wall inside, and a small jetty sticking out beyond it into the lake.* **Swallows and Amazons**

Cormorant Island. *There were plenty of other islands on the lake, but this was one they had not noticed, because it was very small, and so near the mainland that they had thought it was a promontory.* **Swallows and Amazons**

lawn is a boathouse bearing a painted skull and cross-bones. Lanehead itself and Tent Lodge, a little further up the lake, are strong candidates, but neither are anywhere near a river, although Ransome's drawings do have a look of Tent Lodge. A third candidate is Town Head, near Fell Foot Park at the south of Windermere. It bears a strong resemblance to Ransome's drawing, and he would have enjoyed the play on words Town Head and Beckfoot. Just across the lake from Peel Island is a boathouse belonging to Oxen House, a grey stone house that stands beside Torver Beck. It is possible that Ransome took the idea of a house beside a river from Oxen House and then moved the boathouse into the river itself to lead the Swallows towards the fun of Octopus lagoon. The Amazon River itself is Ransome's beloved Crake, and a quarter of a mile downstream is Octopus Lagoon masquerading under the name of Allan Tarn. Because Ransome wanted the Swallows to sail northwards on their cutting-out expedition to the Amazon River, the current is reversed so that the river flows into the lake.

Wild Cat Island. *John steered to pass between the island and the mainland, not too near the island so as not to lose the wind.* **Swallows and Amazons**

After that famous first meeting of the Swallows and Amazons, it is the changing relationship between the Swallows and the houseboat man, now revealed as Nancy and Peggy's Uncle Jim, alias Captain Flint, which gives energy to the remainder of the book. At first the Swallows are suspected of putting a firework on the houseboat's roof and then they are accused of the burglary committed by a couple of local lads from Bigland on the night of the war with the Amazons, when Captain Flint's trunk is stolen. Reconciliation comes with Nancy's intervention and admission that it was she who burnt the cabin roof. Captain Flint

finds himself in the Swallows debt when Titty discovers the stolen trunk on Cormorant Island.

Ransome tried several endings to the story. One interesting departure was his experiment of introducing a parallel narrative. After the burglary, Titty and Roger are allowed to row to Cormorant Island in search of the treasure. While they are away, Nancy gives Captain Flint the black spot and he follows her back to Wild Cat Island to make peace. Having found the trunk, Titty leaves Roger on guard while she delivers the news to the others and arrives to find the enemy seated in the camp.

Ransome readily identified Cormorant Island as Silver Holme on Windermere, and there seems no need to question it. Finally, after the storm washes out the island camp, the allies picnic in Horseshoe Cove. There are one or two possible coves on Windermere, that anyone who drifts along in a boat following Evgenia's advice can discover, but the most likely is Lazy Bay on the western shore, south of Grass Holme, although there are further candidates on Coniston.

Those charged with reviewing the book knew nothing of all this, and there were a couple of bizarre mis-readings. Barbara Euphan Todd (author of Worzal Gummidge) thought the book was set in Chichester Harbour, and an anonymous reviewer in *The Scotsman* wrote 'The tale owes its charm to the fact that the children are not really sailing, but playing at being sailors while all the time they are in the garden at home'. Molly Hamilton, who had liked the book from its earliest beginnings, wrote a glowing review for *Time and Tide*:

The Camping Place. *'Anyhow this is the best place for a camp,' said John. 'Let's put the tents up at once.'* **Swallows and Amazons**

Young Adventurers

There is a small, a very small number of books designed for children which can be enjoyed by both children and grown-ups. *Brer Rabbit*, *The Jungle Book*, and *Old Peter's Russian Tales* are ones that spring to my mind, that fill the Bill, for me. Generally speaking, I dislike children's books most when they are meant for grown-ups. Mr. Ransome's new tale is not meant for grown-ups, but if I am any guide, lots of them will, nevertheless, like it a great deal. The only tinge of sadness that crosses my perfect enjoyment (I have read it twice already, by the way) is that born of the fact that I can't, now, enjoy the thrill open to the younger reader, who will, after reading, proceed to master the craft of sailing and set forth on wondrous and perilous adventures like John and Susan, Titty and Roger. They certainly will do that – and parents will send them forth to it, determined not to fall behind the mother and father of this delightful troupe of sea-men. Sea-men, one says – but the honours go to Able seaman Titty and to the dashing young ladies who manned the ship Amazon; enemies and rivals, at first; later sworn allies in the great campaign against Captain Flint, the master of the house-boat, owner of the parrot, and possessor of the treasure stolen from him – a theft of which Swallows are most unjustly suspected.

The action is genuinely exciting: with very real skill, Mr. Ransome has devised a mimic war whose incidents move with an absorbing tension. Even more attractive – at all events to the older reader – are the actors. Admirably characterized, the four Swallows do definitely belong to one family and at the same time stand out, perfectly individualized. They are more like one another than any one of them is like either of the Amazons, and that distinction most delicately established, is held, right to the end. At the same time, they are quite distinct per-

The Hidden Harbour. *'There are rocks on each side under water,' said Titty.* **Swallows and Amazons**

The Hidden Harbour. *'What a place,' said the able-seaman. 'I expect somebody hid on the island hundreds of years ago, and kept his boat here.'*
Swallows and Amazons

sons – the actions and speeches of Susan, for example, could never be confused with those of Titty. Titty, of course, is the star part; her experiences, alone on the island, like her heroic capture of the Amazons' boat, at a moment when it looks as though the battle between the two crews was helplessly lost, by Swallows (this reader, at any rate, is shamelessly on the side of Swallows), are the high points in the story; it is Titty, again, who finds the treasure on Cormorant Island, and restoring it to Captain Flint seals the friendship with which the great war on the houseboat closes. Titty is a delicious little person, and one hopes, greatly, to meet her again.

The other element that will fascinate both children and adults – the former unconsciously, the latter consciously – is the atmosphere of the book. The romance of a lake, fringed with trees, dotted with islands, steeps the whole book. It is nowhere set down in so many words; yet it pervades the whole atmosphere. One sees the sky and feels the breeze, the more acutely that they are, somehow, suggested, but never described. With the result that to read *Swallows and Amazons* is perfect escape from the here and now: in that sense a holiday, in itself.

Look Out Point. *For a long time after breakfast was over and washing up done they kept watch on Look Out Point on the coming of the Amazon.*
Swallowdale

Rio Bay. *They turned the corner at the bottom. There was the sparkling water of the bay with its landing-stages and its anchored yachts.* **Pigeon Post**

Rio Bay. *She [Amazon] was not in Rio Bay. Four pairs of eyes searched every little jetty.* **Swallows and Amazons**

Bowness Boatmen's Huts. Among the names over the doors of these Victorian huts is that of John Walker, visible in the original of this 1950s photograph.

Chapter Three

Developments and D.'s

No sooner was *Swallows and Amazons* in print, than Ransome was planning its successor. Furthermore, Cape told him not to waste time on anything else but to hurry on with the 'follow-up' and the Altounyans in Aleppo were clamouring to know 'what happens to us next'.

Soon after *Swallows and Amazons* was published, Ransome went to tea with the Kelsall family. Colonel Kelsall was a fishing friend who lived about a mile away across the valley from Low Ludderburn. Desmond Kelsall recalled the occasion.

> I went down to Hartbarrow Bridge to meet him. Walking back from there Arthur Ransome asked if I had enjoyed *Swallows and Amazons*. I said yes, very much, and was he going to write another to follow it. Arthur Ransom said that he was thinking about it. Supposing that he did, what did I think ought to happen in it? With a small boy's typical lack of inhibition I said that I thought that John should become over-confident in handling Swallow and should run her on the rocks. Arthur Ransome gave a great guffaw of laughter and said, 'That's exactly what I was thinking myself, but I haven't got any further than that at the moment.'

Swallowdale, even more than its predecessor, returns to the Lake District of Ransome's youth. It is a land of hound trails, wrestling and village shows, of country life before the impact of tourism. Ransome permitted himself the luxury of allowing the plot to meander through more than 400 pages into which he put his love of the lakes in that lucid and economical style that was born of years of sending despatches from Russia.

The story begins when the Swallows keep their promise to return to Holly Howe the following summer. They set sail for the island where they find a message to say that Captain Flint and his nieces are housebound at Beckfoot where they are entertaining Nancy and Peggy's Great Aunt. The following morning the Swallows sail to Horseshoe Cove to take up their exploration at the point where they had reached the previous year. They are joined by Nancy and Peggy who have escaped in *Amazon* for a few hours. Horseshoe Cove in *Swallowdale* is rather more like one of the bays on the western shore of Coniston Water than Lazy Bay on Windermere. When Titty and Roger have tired of listening to Nancy and Peggy's chatter, they decide to explore by following the beck that runs into the bay.

The landscape has lost the imaginative gloss of *Swallows and Amazons*, but Ransome's lyrical descriptions add greatly to the text:

> The stream was too wide to jump across, but there were places where it was possible to hop from stone to stone and to get across with dry feet if you were lucky. The

Horseshoe Cove. (Windermere) *'What a splendid cove,' said Captain John. 'It's one of our most private haunts,' said Captain Nancy. 'Altogether free of natives.'* **Swallows and Amazons.**

marking every waterfall show that there is only one valley with a pair of falls in this area. Of course Ransome embroidered it with literary camouflage, just as he had done with Wild Cat Island, and gave the valley an abandoned mine borrowed from elsewhere.

The following morning John wrecks *Swallow* on the Pike Rock at the entrance to Horseshoe Cove. Although they salvage her, and with the help of Captain Flint make her fit to sail to the boatyard in Rio Bay, she has to be repaired by boatbuilders. The boatyard is recognisable as Borwick's, that used to be situated at the south side of Bowness Bay.

trees grew close to the stream, and in some places the water had hollowed out a way for itself almost under their roots. There were little pools, foaming at the top where the stream ran in, and smooth and shallow and fast at the hang before it galloped away again down a tiny cataract.

After going under the humpbacked bridge Titty and Roger continue to follow the beck upwards until they reach a waterfall at the foot of a secret valley. It is evident from Clifford Webb's illustration that he was taken to this waterfall, for his drawing is very precise. Swallowdale is to be found somewhere on Blawith Common. It has a Knickerbockerbreaker and an upper waterfall close at hand. Orienteering maps

While she is being repaired, the Swallows have to move camp to the mainland and they settle in the secret valley Titty and Roger found. They are able to use the nearby Swainson's Farm for supplies and messages, and Mary Swainson darns Roger's shorts, just as Annie Swainson had done for young Arthur after he had spent a morning sliding down a nearby Knickerbockerbreaker. In *Swallows and Amazons* a farm was no more than a native settlement, but in *Swallowdale* Swainson's Farm is given its own identity. Its cart-track 'climbed away to the left and came out of the wood by an old white-washed farmhouse with a spring beside it and a stone trough, and a lot of ducks noisily enjoying the overflow from the trough'.

While they are camping in Swallowdale, the Swallows catch fish in Trout Tarn a mile or so above the valley. This is Beacon Tarn that is about the right distance from the secret valley, but the beck mentioned in the book does not link them. Later they cross High Moor on their way to climb Kanchenjunga. Ransome accepted that Kanchenjunga was so easily recognisable as The Old Man of Coniston that he freely gave away its secret. It is less possible to identify High Moor so precisely, for there are several possibilities, but Little Arrow Moor is a strong candidate. They are guided towards the valley of the Amazon by four firs in a line

After their noon-tide owl rendezvous with the Amazons, they all row up the River Amazon, passing beneath not Yewdale Bridge at Coniston but Udal Bridge, until they reach the first cataract: 'a line of low waterfalls that marked the place where the mountain stream changed into the placid little river that wound through meadows to the lake'. At this point also the river Amazon changes from the River Crake to Church Beck, and the Swallows follow the Levers Water branch until they reach the campsite near to the place where the Low Water Beck joins Levers Water Beck. The following morning Nancy leads them across Levers Moss in the direction of the Pudding Stone, and then up the slope of Pudding Cove so as to cross the main path below Low Water before passing between the quarries to reach the summit from the east.

Great Aunt Maria has left and the Amazons are free to join the others in the camp at Swallowdale. Titty and Roger make their way back to Swallowdale by following an unlikely trail of pine cones across the moor, while the others cram into *Amazon*. Roger sprains an ankle and spends the night with the charcoal burners. This gives Ransome another opportunity to bring his old friends, the charcoal burners,

Horseshoe Cove (Coniston). *At the very end of the northern of the two headlands that made the narrow entrance to the cove, a large towel was waving on the top of an oar fixed in the rocks.* **Swallowdale**.

into the story to talk about traditional Lakeland wrestling and the Grasmere Sports.

Swallow is mended at last, but before they all return to Wild Cat Island, the Swallows defeat *Amazon* in a race from the houseboat to the Beckfoot boathouse. The book ends with Susan once more attending to the fire on Wild Cat Island and exclaiming, 'Isn't it a blessing to get home?'

Swallowdale is dedicated to Elizabeth Abercrombie, the daughter of one of his oldest friends, the poet Lascelles Abercrombie. The book was reviewed among the Christmas selection of Naomi Mitchison .

After bewailing the glut of imitation books flooding the market that year, she went on:

Swallowdale is a real book. Probably most children with sensible parents have already had its predecessor, Swallows and Amazons. I think the new one is even better than the old, and the illustrations are admirable, both as showing what happened to John, Susan and the others, and as pictures. It is the kind of book that one discusses in the upper forms of preparatory schools, or even in the lower forms of public schools. It is more real than any of the old children's 'classics' seem now; these boys and girls are far more competent, intelligent and kind than any Victorian or Edwardian family; they have infinitely more dignity and sense of purpose, without having lost either in imagination or adventurousness; they are, m fact, real, modern children, and those who feel gloomy about the future of England should consider that it is boys and girls like the Swallows and Amazons who are the potential new citizens – and there is little to fear! But the main body of readers – those from nine to fourteen – will appreciate it straightforwardly, as an account of adventures to people like themselves, possible, solid, completely satisfying adventures on what must have been the best of all summer holidays.

Memories of the Great Frost of 1895, and the more recent one of 1929, gave Ransome inspiration for his next Lake District book. Furthermore, after attempting to complete the plot with the Swallows and Amazons, he had the brilliant idea of seeing the hard winter and the established characters from the viewpoint of two newcomers. We meet the academic Dick and the literary Dorothea Callum, who are London children of a Professor of Archaeology. In many ways Dick is Arthur himself, a bespectacled young scientist fascinated with natural history, astronomy, chemistry or whatever took his fancy. Similarly Dick's habit of carrying a pocket book with him eat all times came from Ransome himself. Two entries in his note-

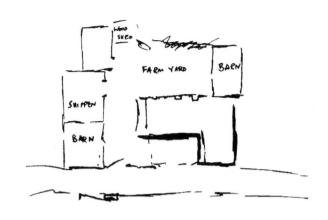

Ransome's sketch plan of Dixon's Farm

book will be familiar to readers of *Winter Holiday*; the first from 1929: 'Light = 186,000 miles per second', and the other from a book started in 1930: 'Mumps from contact 29 days'.

In *Winter Holiday* Ransome must have felt free to borrow the name Dick from Ted Scott's son who survived the boating tragedy that had killed his father on Windermere the previous year. There is a temptation to associate the name with Dick Kelsall, but Ransome, writing in his diaries and elsewhere, called him Richard. Dorothea probably came from Dora (Dorothy) Collingwood, The name was not his first choice, for in an early attempt at the Chapter 'Signalling to Mars' she is called Elizabeth and it is interesting to speculate on the reason for the change of name. It is possible that Ransome's sister Joyce inspired the character, for she also wrote stories in little notebooks and later she wrote children's books. Dorothea lacks Titty's self-confidence, and for much of the time is content to be a follower of others. Only in *The Big Six* does she take the lead in piecing together the evidence that leads to George Owden's downfall. In the three Lake District novels in which Dorothea

Dixon's Farm. *Dick and Dorothea came round the house and out into the road between the garden and a huge barn.* **Winter Holiday.**

appears, Ransome creates some of his most effective images, by allowing the reader to share her viewpoint.

It is the week after Christmas and Dick and Dorothea are staying at Dixon's Farm. Ransome noted privately that Dorothea was aged 11 or 12 and Dick was 10 or 11. Dorothea would have been only a few months younger than Susan and Peggy, and there is a hint of this in the book. On their first morning the newcomers see the Swallows and Amazons on Wild Cat Island and in the afternoon, while they are looking for somewhere for Dick to do his stargazing, they see them again at Holly Howe. Dick suggests signalling to them, but later that evening it is Dorothea who

Rio Boatsheds. *All along the nearer side of Rio Bay were the building yards, where rowing boats were built and little ships like* Swallow *and racing yachts, besides motor boats for the people who did not know how to manage sails.* **Swallowdale**

pushes him into actually doing it. Eventually their signals are seen from 'Mars' and this leads to a meeting the following morning.

Nancy, with typical generosity of spirit, is impressed with the signalling idea and invites them to join in the latest scheme that takes the form of a North Polar Expedition. When it is discovered that the newcomers are excellent skaters they are no longer merely tolerated by the Swallows, but welcomed. The Swallows have everything to learn about skating, and a delightful passage in the book

was inspired by the Altounyan girls learning to skate on Tarn Hows. The girls were at Annisgarth School in Windermere, and Ransome would collect Taqui, Susie and Titty from school in the car that he used to drive round the lanes with such zest that the girls were frequently sick. They visited Low Ludderburn at weekends, sometimes staying for a day or two, and in the great workroom, they were treated to readings of the work in hand and occasionally in summer they were taken sailing.

The barn above Dixon's Farm becomes a signal

station so that the D.'s can receive messages from Holly Howe and join the others each day. The signals were already in use between Low Ludderburn and the barn at Colonel Kelsall's home at Barkbooth. In their final form they could convey 74 messages. Mostly the elaborate system was used for fishing messages, but without leaving the terrace in front of the cottage Evgenia could arrange for the colonel to collect her at a certain time and take her shopping in Windermere. The signals were invaluable on one occasion when Ransome fell ill and Kelsall arrived at the cottage a quarter of an hour after Evgenia had hoisted her S.O.S.

When it is discovered that Nancy has mumps, there is general rejoicing that the others will have an extra month's holiday. Ransome paints a delightful picture of Windermere during one of those rare winters when the lake freezes from end to end. The Arctic explorers are able to camp each day in the houseboat in its new role as the *Fram*, originally the vessel of the Norwegian Arctic explorer Nansen, whom Ransome had met. Captain Flint returns to enjoy the frozen lake and meets the D.'s in a hilarious episode. He is invited to join the expedition's march to the head of the lake to discover the North Pole. There is a breakdown in communication that in these days of mobile phones would never happen, and the D.'s set out for the Pole a day early. They are overtaken by a blizzard and their sailing sledge is blown to the head of the lake before crashing on the shore. They manage to reach the summerhouse that Captain Flint has borrowed to do duty as the North Pole, and the others eventually follow with their relief expeditions.

There has been almost as much speculation about the origin of the North Pole as there has about Swallowdale. People have 'remembered' it at various places and until recently the conservatory extension to Wanless Howe, just above the road running by

Rio Boatbuilders. *There were boathouses and little docks. There were sheds a few yards back from the water, with railway lines running down into the lake, and wheeled carriages resting on the railway lines to carry boats into the water and bring them up out of it.* **Swallowdale.**

Borrans Park (which I photographed in the 1960s), had seemed the most likely inspiration. Then Dick Kelsall claimed that he had seen the very summerhouse in the exact spot at the head of the lake around 1930. A local member of the Arthur Ransome Society, Jim Andrews, confirmed this by dowsing and even found the bow windows of which Ransome spoke. I have seen a demonstration of this dowsing, and most

The North Pole. *It could not be all windows. He found steps and a door. He hammered on it. There was no answer. He turned the handle, the door opened inwards, and he almost fell through it into a small room.* **Winter Holiday** The North Pole was demolished many years ago. This print was made from a frame of an 8mm cine film in 1965.

impressive it is too, for there are a lot of Roman remains in the area to which the dowsing rods also respond. I have tried without success to find supporting evidence for their find. No photographs, large-scale maps of the period or land use surveys that I have studied make any reference to a building at that particular spot. Nor do any of the Waterhead residents questioned remember any building there – and one person's memory went back to 1922. The land belonged to Ambleside Urban District Council, having been purchased by public subscription in 1925. There was however a flagpole at the Wateredge Hotel where the Ransomes used to go for tea.

The inspiration for the North Pole's origin, if not the actual building, seems to have been the Turret Room at Brantwood overlooking Coniston Water and Coniston Old Man, where John Ruskin lived for 29 years until his death in 1900. Ruskin could very well

Clifford Webb's illustration of the Swallowdale waterfall

have been, the old man who, having built it, 'could look out on the changing scenery and its enclosing hills. He could sit there watching the lake in storm and be himself most comfortable behind windows that could be thrown open in the heat of summer.' Until some supporting evidence is available, it still seems more likely that the old conservatory at Wanlass Howe, high above the road round the head of

Swallowdale Waterfall. *They hurried on until they stood below the waterfall. Above them the water poured noisily from ledge to ledge of rock, and they could get no further without climbing up the rocks beside the falling water.* **Swallowdale**

the lake, was the nearest approximation to the building itself. It fits the two finished drawings in *Winter Holiday* which show the North Pole situated above the explorers and not on the almost flat ground of Borrans Park.

When *Winter Holiday* was published its reviewers did not felt cheated because the Swallows were not the central characters, as Ransome had feared. An anonymous reviewer for *The Times Literary Supplement* wrote:

A very different kind of book, though it also deals with the adventures of a party of children in the snowy season of the year, is *Winter Holiday*, by Arthur Ransome

(Jonathan Cape, 7s 6d net). Those who read *Peter Duck* last year have been looking forward eagerly to Mr Ransome's next story, and we can promise them that they will not be disappointed. They must be warned, however, that although *Winter Holiday* is about the same children who appeared in *Peter Duck* (with two new children added) it differs from that enchanting story in an important particular. In last year's book the children had an adventure which every grown-up person would say could not have happened to them in present-day life. It is true that it was related with such convincing realism that only a grown-up who had never been a child could fail to be carried away by it when actually reading the book: but after laying it down most parents probably rubbed their eyes, said that it must all have been a dream or a "make up" and discouraged their offspring from hoping for similar adventures. But no one can say that *Winter Holiday* is improbable. It is about some boys and girls who were spending a part of the Christmas holidays near one of the English lakes, and who were detained for an extra month by quarantine for mumps. Every parent of schoolchildren will recognize the severe realism of the details about health certificates. Yet it is full of a strange glamour which imaginative people of all ages will feel. In reading it we see the landscape and the events through the eyes of the characters in the book. Young readers will find themselves taking part in signalling to the Martians and going to the North Pole, and old readers will be carried back in their minds to those wonderful games of childhood when the whole world of everyday things was doubled with another more glam-

Beckfoot *Beyond the boathouse was the old grey house of Beckfoot.* **Pigeon Post**

orous world into which they could transport themselves at a moment's notice and in which they led a heroic life. Miss Nancy Blackett's charming illustrations contribute a great deal to the fascination of the book; she is herself one of the characters in the story, and makes us see how things looked to them. One could hardly have a better story about children.

After visiting the Norfolk Broads in *Coot Club*,

Ransome returned to the Lake District and another land-based adventure in 1935.

The story starts at the beginning of the following summer holidays. Titty and Roger arrive by train at Strickland Junction, easily recognisable from the text as Oxenholme, but disguised by the mirror-drawing used as a frontispiece. Here they find a pigeon basket awaiting their collection. After releasing the pigeon,

Ransome's preliminary sketch for an unused illustration of Beckfoot.

Nancy's disgust. Captain Flint has gone to South America on a mining trip. She decides that if they could find gold in the fells, he would not go gallivanting off just when she wants him aboard the houseboat to join in her games. She takes them all up the Amazon River and part way up Kanchenjunga into a tunnel where an old miner, Slater Bob, confirms that there is gold to be found in the fells.

An entry in Ransome's diary for 1929 noted that Oscar Gnosspelius had found copper on Coniston Old Man. Gnosspelius was an old family friend who had married Barbara Collingwood after a varied career which included civil engineering in Africa and South America and various forms of aero engineering (he designed and built a float plane that took off from Windermere). They settled at High Hollin Bank, a little distance from Lanehead. Copper had been mined in the Coniston fells for over three hundred years, but since the beginning of the century attempts to find economically workable copper veins had been sporadic and short-lived. This one was similarly unsuccessful, and by the time Ransome was writing *Pigeon Post* it had been abandoned.

John (Willie) Shaw inspired Slater Bob and his mine, known as Horse Crag Level, is at Tilberthwaite, not far from the bridge. The mine is just as Ransome described it, with a long tunnel leading to a chamber which was built originally as a drain for the copper mine and reopened for slate – much as Slater Bob told the prospectors. When Oscar Gnosspelius abandoned his attempt to mine for copper in 1933 he set up Shaw at Horse Crag Level, and there he remained until he retired in 1938.

Old Bob tells them of gold that is to be found somewhere on the other side of the mountain, much to the consternation of Mrs Blackett who does not want them charging around all over the country while there is such a high risk of fell fires at the end of a long

they continue their journey to Windermere where they are met by Nancy and her mother in Rattletrap. Almost certainly, this was based Ransome's open Trojan car that he had been driving for a while. They arrive at Beckfoot to find the Swallows, Amazons and D.'s camping in the Beckfoot garden. This sad state of affairs is because Mrs Blackett wants to keep them within reach until Mrs Walker comes to Holly Howe and they can return to Wild Cat Island. Much to dry summer. Eventually, after they arrange to camp beside a farm at the head of the valley and send a pigeon with a message every day to say that they are all well, she capitulates. The ingenious contrivance by which the pigeons are made to ring a bell in the Beckfoot hall as they enter the pigeon loft across the stable yard was the work of Dick Kelsall. He and his brother and the Hudson girls helped Ransome with some more hollywoods for the illustrations.

Having left the gear at the farm with Mrs Tyson, they climb the steep track to the gold fields that Ransome called High Topps. This country has been cleverly disguised by creating it in the mirror image of reality. Yewdale Beck above Shepherd's Bridge is the upper reaches of the River Amazon with its winding, undulating road and a bridge over the beck at Tilberthwaite leading to a farm. To the south of the beck is the high rocky plateau under the shoulder of Wetherlam that Ransome chose for his gold fields. It is confirmed by a

Charcoal Burners' Hut. *All the Swallows were staring at the hut. 'It's a Red Indian's wigwam,' said Titty.* **Swallowdale**

diary entry for 27th March 1935 when he went up behind Tilberthwaite with 'Gnossie', to see several of the old copper workings and 'a suitable bit of country for my story'. Gnosspelius showed Ransome the proper way to crush and pan for golddust and how to use a blowpipe – skills essential to the development of the story.

When Titty finds water by dowsing in an old charcoal burner's pitstead on the edge of High Topps they can all move nearer to their work. A stranger, whom

the prospectors call Squashy Hat, is suspected of being a rival as he studies his map and paints white spots marking a vein of copper on the slopes. Squashy Hat was based on Gnosspelius himself as Ransome's family and friends were quick to spot. Eventually, Roger discovers the gold while indulging in a private game and John and Nancy insist on proper crushing and panning in order that Captain Flint may be greeted with a nugget of pure gold on his return. The younger ones are instructed to watch

Charcoal Burning. *'We want ours to burn good and slow,' said Young Billy. 'Once he's got a good hold you can cover the fire up and the better you cover him the hotter he is and the slower he burns.'* **Swallowdale**

Squashy Hat and see that he keeps well away from their mine. They become trapped in a tunnel from which their rival has just emerged when 'The Old Level' collapses behind them. Thanks to Dick's good sense and cool head, they are able to escape through the mountain to Slater Bob's. It was once possible to go from High Topps to Slater Bob's in reality, but as it involved a descent of 500 feet, it was not just a simple matter of walking along tunnels. In June, Gnosspelius

was helping again, taking Ransome up Swallow Scar above Grey Screes. It was 'very jolly up there above the screes', wrote Ransome, who watched peregrine falcons.

The blast furnace is a disaster and the young prospectors are almost burnt by a fell fire before Captain Flint returns at last and they discover that what they have found is a rich vein of copper. This turns out to be exactly what Captain Flint and his shy friend, the rival prospector who had returned early, had been looking for all the time.

The most interesting review of *Pigeon Post* was that of M.E. Atkinson. Mary Atkinson had her first children's book, *August Adventure,* published the same year by Jonathan Cape, and she was one of the first writers to be strongly influenced by Ransome.

Susan, John, Titty, Roger and, of course, the Blacketts – they are all back with us in *Pigeon Post*. We enjoyed *Coot Club*: but old friends are best. It is good, too, to return to the lake country. Here is a fine yarn – with an excellent plot. Ransome 'fans' will be glad to hear it has his own illustrations. It was disgusting of me to guess the identity of 'Squashy Hat'. But should the young be equally discerning, it will not spoil their enjoyment of the story any more than it did mine, for the inspiring companionship of Nancy Blackett can create thrill where thrill does not truly exist.

Pigeon Post is an inland story, the story of a Gold Rush. Gold – in the lakes? Alas, it was another mineral. But as its presence was equally welcome to Captain Flint, no one need be disappointed. Our prospectors, after all, had but one end in view – the discovery of something that should serve to keep their wandering friend anchored in home waters, and make up to him for the failure of his own prospecting overseas. Captain Flint being on his way home from the Gold Rush is a rush against time. There is one snag: the gold fields are miles away among the Fells. How can one allow the children to camp at such a distance? But, after all, one had to consider Susan's reliability, Dick's ingenuity, and – the homing pigeons. Every day reassuring messages fly to Beckfoot, their arrival announced by a marvellous gadget of Dick's contriving. Friends of the two D.'s will be cheered to find the inclusion of Dick and Dorothea in the party. It is Dick who takes the lead in the scientific part of the mining activities. Budding engineers will enjoy his many contraptions.

Boys may consider the piratical Nancy too much of a good thing. They must remember she is as nearly a boy (a pirate-boy) as she knows how. The convert is ever more of a fanatic than he that is born within the fold. Compared with her, the solid masculinity of John is cooling to the brow.

Children like the reality of detail, and here Mr Ransome excels: there is plenty, and a little more. Nor are the big thrills lacking: vide the falling-in of the tunnel, the finding of the 'gold', Titty's water-divining (the best thing in the book), the night with the blast-furnace, the heath fire. Boys and girls will always relish Arthur Ransome's stories to the full, because they are about themselves. All their adventures are possible for children.

And now one genuine complaint. Why has this author (whose first published work appeared in 1909) waited until recent years to write those unique books? I was a child in 1909. It isn't fair.

The Picts and the Martyrs is the shortest of the entire canon and it brought forth the fiercest criticism from Evgenia. The story opens at the beginning of the summer holidays with Nancy and Peggy alone at Beckfoot while their mother recuperates from an illness. Captain Flint has taken her on a cruise that somehow the Great Aunt comes to hear about and she decides it is her duty to take over the household. To make matters worse, the D.'s have just arrived. By now, Ransome's private note reveals that Dorothea was aged 13, Dick 12, Nancy 15 and Peggy 14. Nancy realises that the G.A. thinks her mother is being irresponsible and will be even more cross with her on her return, if she finds that they have been allowed to have visitors. The only solution is for the D.'s to lie hid for the duration of her visit in an old hut called The Dogs' Home in the nearby woods. There is just such a hut among the Forestry Commission woodlands north of Ransome's old home at The Heald. The name has puzzled a number of people, but among the end-paper advertisements in the diary that Ransome bought each year, there is the Battersea Dogs' Home panel, headed boldly 'The Dogs' Home'.

To complicate matters, the D.'s are expecting to sail their new boat that they have named *Scarab* after the sacred beetle of the ancient Egyptians. *Scarab* was based on Ransome's own dinghy, *Coch-y-bonddhu*. Dick is also to help with the analysis of the copper samples from the mine which Captain Flint's partner, Timothy, hopes to complete before his return. Dorothea has to learn housekeeping and Dick has to master handling a new boat in order to do everything they had planned, and yet remain hidden for almost a fortnight. In the end Nancy's plan succeeds in spite of complications caused by Dick's 'burglary' of Beckfoot and the Great Aunt's fixation that the Swallows are around somewhere.

The Picts and the Martyrs is the ultimate development of Ransome's fictional Lake District. The local folk are no longer regarded as quaint exotics labelled 'savages', as they had been by the imaginative Titty in *Swallows and Amazons*, but have become three-dimensional and as much a part of the scene as the great hills. Ever since their arrival at Dixon's Farm in *Winter Holiday*, the D.'s have related to the local people in a way the Swallows do not, except perhaps Roger and old Mr Swainson and later Young Billy. In *The Picts and the Martyrs*, Jacky the farm boy is central to the D.'s successful survival in the hut in the wood and a reminder that Ransome himself had learnt from the country people as a young man and during his boyhood holidays at Nibthwaite. On the night of her arrival, Dorothea's response: 'There isn't a lovelier place in all the world,' sets the tone for the book which became Ransome's final expression of his love affair with the Lake District of his youth and its most complete evocation.

Mary Treadgold, a distinguished fellow Cape author, wrote an enthusiastic review:

One day in a Ransome moves with the rapidity of panzer warfare. After the ten-day span of *The Picts and the Martyrs* I regained my breath with the old dizzy, delighted feeling engendered by a double go on the Giant Racer. After all these years of continuous publication, events in the Ransome books still move freshly and excitingly, in *The Picts and the Martyrs* once again to the pace and urgency of Nancy's ferociously inventive brain, with Dick and Dorothea as usual stumbling a little uncertainly in her wake. Even at the end when we are all of us in a condition of crowing, gasping exhaustion, only a pause is hinted.

'"Yes," said Nancy with a new look in her eyes. And only ten days gone after all. And now we're free to start stirring things up. We'll hoist the skull and crossbones again the moment we've had our grub. We'll get things moving without wasting a minute."'

After the wild doings in the far China seas with Missee Lee last Christmas twelvemonth, I was glad to be back in the smaller preoccupations of Beckfoot. Nancy and Peggy Blackett entertaining the two D.'s in the absence of their mother. 'he that cannot contract the sight of his mind as well as disperse and dilate wanteth a great faculty,' said Bacon. For ingenuity of plot-development on a small scale, for the raising of a Kanchenjunga of complications infinitesimal in importance to all but the few involved, *The Picts and the Martyrs* easily passes the post first among the Ransomes. Almost with the opening pages the decorous docility promised by Nancy to her absent mother is wrecked by the unexpected arrival of a Great aunt – to quote Cook, a 'girt auld hen 'at wants to cock o' t' midden'. The GA is not expected to be tolerant of visitors, and the two D.'s are banished by Nancy to be Picts in a stone hut in the woods, while Nancy and Peggy give themselves over to a *Via Dolorosa* of Martyrdom ('Soap and water. White frocks. Oh gosh, and party shoes.') Thence and onward the network of deception and counter-deception spread by the Picts in the Hut and the Martyrs in the House, is hourly, minutely, rendered more complex by the ruthless attentions of Nancy, who in dreadful energy, makes bad unnecessarily worse until the train finally back to the waters of Harrogate.

As usual I finished, loving to the last page that perpetual expectancy of adventure in all those Ransome children – whether it is Nancy's young eager grasping of the moment, the more cautious assessment and acceptance of events by the two D.'s, or the unmoved, unsurprised acquiescent detachment of the country child, Jacky – a new and endearing character. Almost I could wish that these children – living tirelessly at their own arduous pace against a background of shadowy grown-ups and with hills and trees as greater realities than these – were the people to entrust our own coming adventures – adventures like the Beveridge Plan. *The Picts and The Martyrs* could still teach our statesmen to live imaginatively.

For a dozen years Ransome had been storing up the idea for a Victorian tale about 'an old schoolmaster and a fisherman and a boy and a river', a *Bevis*-like novel based on Tom Stainton, the water bailiff of the River Beela. He called it *The River Comes First* and wrote several chapters of narrative and, despite greatly improving it when he abandoned the attempt to tell it in the first person, he finally gave up. Evgenia's strong opposition must have had some bearing on the decision, but what he did write shows that Ransome's power of imagery was undiminished:

> The gamekeeper's cottage stood where it stands today set back in the edge of the wood and looking out over the straight bit of the river that is known as Long Dub. Some of the trees have grown since then, but others have been cut, and probably it was then much as it is now, sheltered by the wood from the south-west wind and catching the morning sun across the river. It was a two-storied cottage, rough cast and white-washed, with a slate-roofed porch covered with a climbing rose that had been planted on the gamekeeper's wedding day, a present to Tom's mother from the old gardener at the hall. In fourteen years it had covered the porch and was spreading over the side of the house, all but framing the window of the kitchen. It was one of those roses that

find it hard to make up their minds to stop flowering, and it was Mary Staunton's pride that in all but the hardest winters she was able to pick a bud from it, and have it blossom in the house on Christmas Day. Inside the porch, over the door, there was nailed the antler of a deer, from which hung an old cowbell, with a string to the clapper of it and a fox's pad to the end of that, a handle for anybody who wanted to ring the bell.

Similarly in this description of the river during a drought:

> The river was dead low, stones showing that I'd never seen above water, moss on the flats and hardly a stir in the pools. You could see the fish crossing the shallows with their back fins out … Fainting hot it was, with no wind and never a stir in the reflections but for a trout. Looking up the river, you could see every tree and leaf in the water above the ford, and looking across to the wood it was the same and the sun coming off the water like a warming pan held to your face.

Ransome tried to bring his Norfolk boys – central characters in *Coot Club* and *The Big Six* – to visit the D.'s and their friends on the lake in the unfinished story that Hugh Brogan discovered while researching his *Life of Arthur Ransome*. It had no title and Brogan called it *Coots in the North*. It was finally published in 1988, together with a number of other Ransome short stories, including two self-contained passages from *The River Comes First*. *Coots in the North* tells how Joe, Bill and Pete secretly stowed away on board a cruiser being transported to Rio, where they met Nancy and Peggy clowning about on the lake. The Swallows and D.'s are in close attendance, but here the story peters out, although Ransome left a clear outline for the remainder of the book.

He took the setting of his fishing holidays in the Hebrides for the last of the series, *Great Northern?* The plot was suggested by his friend, Myles North and brought the Swallows, Amazons and D.'s into conflict with a determined, but eventually unsuccessful egg collector intent on stealing the eggs of the first great northern diver to nest in Britain. *Great Northern?* is best enjoyed as a fantasy like *Peter Duck* and *Missee Lee.*

The series properly reaches its conclusion at the end of *The Picts and the Martyrs* with the Swallows due to arrive and Nancy, about to hoist the skull and crossbones on the Beckfoot promontory, reminding everyone that there are '… five whole weeks of the holiday still to go.'

The Beckfoot Promontory. *'Over there, beyond the islands, running out into the lake on the far side. No, further along. Woods behind, at the back of it, then just heather and rock.'* **Winter Holiday**.

Darning Roger

Swainson's Farm. *Mary darned him about twice a day until at last he was tired of the 'Knickerbockerbreaker', which Titty said, was much the best name for it.'* **Swallowdale**

The River Amazon. *Again there was a splash in the deep reed beds at the river's mouth. Again a duck quacked loudly. It quacked two or three times until a voice said sternly, 'Stow it, you goat. Don't overdo things.'* **Swallows and Amazons**

Octopus Lagoon. *'Here's the lagoon,' said Susan, and the boat shot out into a small lake almost covered by big patches of broad-leaved water lilies. Even in daylight it was hard not to catch them with the oars.* **Swallowdale.**

Trout Tarn. *Trout Tarn was nearly a mile beyond Swallowdale, high on the top of the moor, a little lake lying in a hollow of rock and heather. When the Swallows saw it, they wished almost that they had made their camp on its rocky shores.* **Swallowdale.**

High Moor. *Already the peak of Kanchenjunga began to look as if it had been cut out of dark purple cardboard. To the right and to the left of it were other hills, and somewhere over the edge of the moor the explorers knew they would find the valley of the Amazon River.* **Swallowdale**

Kanchenjunga Beck. *The stream hurrying down from Kanchenjunga fell more steeply than the little beck that had led the able-seaman and the boy to the discovery of Swallowdale. It dropped sometimes ten, twenty feet at a time into pools from which the white foam spurted high in the air to meet it.* **Swallowdale.**

The Half-way Camp. *To the left the peak of Kanchenjunga rose above the lesser crags that curved about the head of the ravine. Far up among those they could see thin white lines where the becks were still carrying water collected on the tops. To right and left were rough fells through which it seemed that the little stream at their feet had carved a channel fit for a river a thousand times bigger than itself.* **Swallowdale.**

Climbing Kanchenjunga. *There were things to shout, such as 'Don't touch this rock. It's a loose one,' but mostly it was grim straight-ahead, silent climbing.* **Swallowdale.**

The Summit Cairn. *It was not until they were actually standing beside the cairn that marked the highest point of Kanchenjunga, that they could see what lay beyond the mountain. Then indeed they knew they were on the roof of the world.* **Swallowdale**

The Swallows and Amazons saw wild goats on the summit. One year we found some very tame sheep.

Dow Crag. *'Due west from here,' said John, looking at the compass in his hand. It's the Isle of Man.'* **Swallowdale.** Sadly, the Isle of Man, though visible to the naked eye, has not registered on the photograph.

Snow in Rio Bay. *There was a new world. Everything was white and somehow still. Everything was holding its breath.* **Winter Holiday.** (Photo: Michael Wilson)

Frozen Windermere. *The last occasion when Windermere really froze was in 1929.* (Photo: courtesy Ed Geddard)

The Station. *A smallish ancient motor-car had driven into the station yard. Mrs Blackett, round, small, no taller than Nancy was talking to the porter.* **Pigeon Post**

Arrival. *'Books were hurriedly stowed away. Dorothea wrote "Arrived safely. Dick and Dorothea" on the addressed postcard her mother had given her to be sent off from the station. The train jerked to a standstill.'* **The Picts and the Martyrs.**

Ransome's preliminary sketch.

Slater Bob talks of Gold

Inside Slater Bob's. *They were at the mouth of a lofty chamber in the rock. The dazzling light of the acetylene lamp that hung from an iron spike driven into a crack in the rock showed them a short broad-shouldered old man leaning on a baulk of timber that he had been shaping with an axe.*
Pigeon Post (Photo: Ted Alexander)

The Igloo. *A low hut with no windows looking almost like a heap of stones.* **Winter Holiday.**

The Amazon River. *Their own road was narrow and winding, going up the valley close to the dried-up little river.* **Pigeon Post.**

Tyson's Farm. *A narrow lane turned to the right out of the road, crossed the almost dry bed of the river by a small hump-backed stone bridge, and ended in the cobbled yard of a whitewashed farmhouse. On one side of the yard was the house itself, with low windows and a porch with clematis climbing over it, a big cowhouse with a barn above it and an old pump with a shallow drinking trough.* **Pigeon Post.**

High Topps. *'Well, what do you think of it?' said Nancy waving her arm as if she had somehow herself conjured the whole of High Topps into existence.* **Pigeon Post.**

The Dogs' Home. *They came to the place where the beck crossed the path. 'Hello,' said Peggy. 'Somebody's put down stepping stones. There never used to be any.'*
On the other side of the beck some of the trees had been cleared long ago and in the open space was an ancient old hut, built of rough stones.
The Picts and the Martyrs.

The River at The Head Of The Lake. *'There's a stile into the road by that bridge. And houses quite near. Let's go and look for that bookshop and something to eat.'* **The Picts and the Martyrs.**

The *Tern*. *The steamer with a great flurry of reversed propellers, was coming alongside the pier.* **The Picts and the Martyrs.**

Chapter Four

The Best of Childhood?

Writing in his favourite workroom with its glorious view across the Winster valley towards Yorkshire in 1934, Ransome claimed:

> Writing is one profession in which one can have one's cake and eat it, and it seems to me that in writing children's books, I have the best of childhood over again and the best of being old as well, which is a very great deal more than I deserve.

The Swallows, Amazons and D.'s became very real to Ransome and there is little doubt that their creation gratified him. Those who knew him at that time have told how he spoke of the children as if they really existed. Their adventures appealed to the eternal boy in his make up, yet the literary craftsman in him also needed to be satisfied and he was torn between meeting his publisher's deadlines and reaching his own high standards – and those of his wife; his fiercest critic. Readers can judge for themselves to what extent his assertion was an amiable white lie.

Ransome's diary entry for March 24 1929 states simply, 'Began *S and A*'. Only the previous week, after much deliberation, he had thrown up his steady job with the *Manchester Guardian* and given three months notice, after C.P. Scott, the editor, had asked him to go to Berlin as resident correspondent on a greatly increased salary. On completion of this tour of duty he would be allowed to return to Manchester and become Literary Editor. Ransome realised that his life was at the crossroads. Never having wanted to become a journalist, and aware of the demands that such a career would make, he knew that if he accepted the offer he would probably not be able to write another book. Finally, Evgenia and he courageously decided that a financially uncertain future was a better one than being slowly strangled by politics and journalism. They decided that in future he would work for the paper only on a freelance basis. Having travelled to Manchester to break the news, the Ransomes took *Swallow* from the Borwick's boatshed in Bowness Bay and went for their first sail. In one account, Ransome wrote that it was during that sail that he had the idea of writing a book in which the heroine would be the little boat itself.

For the previous four years he had been at the beck and call of the newspaper that had sent him abroad whenever the political situation called for somebody to assess the state of affairs on the spot and send back authoritative despatches. The year 1928 had been a typically busy one. Ransome had spent the month of February in Russia, and since his return had written 43 of his celebrated 'Rod and Line' fishing essays for the *Manchester Guardian*, compiled 49 reviews and produced eight political leaders. The duodenal ulcer that had first begun to trouble him in Russia, had become worse, and it was against this background that he wrote to his mother at Christmas, 'I'd like to send you a new book by myself. But I haven't written one and have begun to feel I never shall again.'

A couple of pages of notes hidden away in the notebook he later used as the log for his yacht *Nancy Blackett*, reveal some of his first thoughts. The note makes it clear that the names John, Nancy and Peggy were not his first choice, but that he had already decided upon the names Susan, Titty and Roger.

Swallows	~~Dick~~ John 12	Amazons	Jane 13
Susan 10			Mary (proper name Ruth) 12
Titty 8			Tom 3
Roger 6			
Vic Does not count			
Parents to Amazons ~~Smith~~		Walker	
Mother of the Swallows		Smith	
The Houseboat Man		Turner	

It is interesting to note that John Walker was originally Dick Smith! The rejected name of Dick is an interesting choice and suggests Dick Scott, the son of his closest friend. The boy visited Ludderburn occasionally and had been staying there a day or so before the Altounyans arrived with their birthday gift. He was introduced to fishing and sailing by Ransome and was about twelve years old at the time.

On another page Ransome made a list of chapters:

1. Introductory. Tents & Swallow
2. Preparation. —————————- & collecting outfit
3. Island. First landing
4. Cormorants. Fishing. The Houseboat man. Mother after a sleep.
5. An enemy. The Amazons. The Amazon.. Jane, Ruth (crossed out) Mary

(Ruthless)

6. Tame without the Amazons. Dick going home. Take the Post. Agreement with mother.
7. The lighthouse and lights.
8. The expedition.
9. Titty alone. The wrong boat.
10. The Amazons on the island. Titty in the boat.
11. ————————————— ——————————— Peace with the Amazons.
12. Dick learns of burgled houseboat. Did he do it?
13. Search party conquered by the children who rescue them hospitably.
14. Policeman (crossed out)
15. Titty & the treasure from the houseboat.
16. The second arrow. 'We are prisoners.'
17. The rescue.
18. The Amazons' captive. entertainment by the children. The letter with thanks
19. The discovery of thieves by the children. The number of the car. All help to ——————-
20. The end.

This is followed by a list of books: *Baltic Pilot*, a German Dictionary, *Brown's Signalling Manual*, *The Mate's Handybook* and *Simple Cooking for Small Households*. A note found with the draft dated 1929, indicates how his thoughts advanced:

Swallows	John 12	Amazons	~~Jane~~
Susan 10		Nancy 13	
Titty 9		~~Mary~~	
Roger 7		Peggy 12	
Victoria (Bridget)		Tom 3	

In 1926 his friend Molly Hamilton tried to interest Jonathan Cape in Ransome's children's fantasy, *The Blue Treacle*, written for his daughter Tabitha. Mrs Hamilton who became an MP, a representative on the League of Nations and a Governor of the BBC was one of Ransome's closest friends. Cape was not to be persuaded. Instead, he tried to commission Ransome to write a literary biography, as he thought it high time that he published another book. Early in 1929, Cape agreed to publish a collection of the best of the 'Rod and Line' essays. On April 5th, Ransome travelled to London where he showed the first fifty pages of 'The Swallows and The Amazons' to Molly Hamilton, and encouraged by her good opinion, took half a page of notes and a list of chapter headings for 'The Swallows and the Amazons' to Jonathan Cape. Cape agreed to publish the book, though he made it clear that what he really wanted was the promised collection of essays. Cape's copy of the contract has survived. It is very simple by today's standards, agreeing to pay ten per cent on the first five thousand copies and fifteen per cent thereafter; with an advance of £100 payable on the day of publication.

The following day Ransome celebrated by fishing with friends at Droxford in Hampshire. Then he returned to Ludderburn and, swept along in a rush of enthusiasm, continued to work on the first draft of *Swallows and Amazons*, begrudging time spent on anything else.

In each of his diaries from 1929 until 1946 Ransome constructed a matrix in which he wrote the number of pages that he had written or revised that day. From these entries it is possible to follow the ebb and flow of his output, and see the periods when he was able to surge ahead and the times when the book just would not go for him. On 13th April he wrote four pages of 'The First Arrow', and followed this with three pages of 'The Parley', reaching a total of 64

pages completed. On 18th May, just eight weeks after he had started, the story was complete. Never again would he be able to complete a first draft with such ease. It is little wonder that he said that the book 'almost wrote itself'! He had planned for 200 pages of typescript, but by the time he had finished he had reached page 253.

The revision began in early June and Ransome made good progress although he continued with 'Rod and Line' essays for the *Manchester Guardian*. In July his great friend Ted Scott at last took over as editor of the paper, and Ransome was unable to refuse his request for regular Saturday articles on a wide variety of topics of his own choosing. Once Ransome turned his attention on the Saturday articles, he found the chore of turning out a weekly essay of around 2000 words much more difficult and worrying than he expected. Meanwhile, 'Rod and Line' continued until September. It is hardly surprising that in these circumstances the revision of *Swallows and Amazons* came to a halt.

The book was saved when Ransome was sent to Egypt at the end of November in order to cover the General Election. When he fell ill in Cairo it proved to be a b1essing in disguise, because he was able to forge ahead with the revision from his sickbed. Once started, the revision continued when he returned at the beginning of February. Ivor Brown, who had deputized for him as writer of the Saturday articles while he was abroad, continued until the end of the month.

The first 238 pages were sent to Cape in the middle of March while Ransome worked on a couple of chapters near the finish, and by the end of the month the book was complete. He described the writing in his draft entitled, *How Swallows and Amazons Came to be Written* which was published in the United States to coincide with the American edition:

I was enjoying the writing of this book more than I have ever enjoyed writing any other book in my life. And I think I can put my figure on the thing in it which gave me so much pleasure, it was just this, the way in which the children in it have no firm dividing line between make-believe and reality, but slip in and out of one and the other again and again.

But the book still required illustrations, for it was almost unheard of for a child's book in those days to be without pictures. Cape commissioned Stephen Spurrier, and Ransome visited the artist in Chichester. In the event, he strongly disapproved of Spurrier's drawings, and only the endpaper map, the Wild Cat Island map and the title page vignette appeared in the book. There is no record of what Spurrier thought of all this.

Jonathan Cape's partner G. Wren Howard looked after Ransome and their association was a long and fruitful one. Towards the end of Ransome's life, when he was unable to deal with his correspondence, Wren Howard took over the task of answering letters from fans on his behalf. Wren Howard's first surviving letter was very much to the point:

I am naturally very disturbed by the fact that you dislike the illustrations or most of them so much, though actually I am not altogether surprised. Personally, I believe that most of them would look very much better when reduced and reproduced, but it seems to me that it is not the slightest use going on with even a selection from them when you don't really like any of them at all. Frankly, I don't really believe that any illustrations would please you and with that point of view I heartily sympathise ...

I am writing to Spurrier – obviously not a pleasant job – and will break it to him as gently as I can. I am afraid that by now he will have done most of the drawings and of course we shall have to pay him the same fee as if we had used the drawings. I have a warned the printer that there will be no illustrations, which, from

one point of view, will be an advantage because the book, as you know, is long.

Of course the absence of illustrations will almost certainly make the book more difficult to sell, to start with at any rate, and we shall have to try to make up for the lack of illustrations with a very intensive campaign to influence, if we can, the reviewers. Of course if a certain number them can be persuaded to come forward and review the book and at length, the day will probably be won.

I enclose proofs of the endpapers and map and hope to heaven you will like these. I believe that in this case you will be satisfied because at rate, to my unpractised eye, both drawings seem me intriguing and the right sort of stuff for the job.

Spurrier was an accomplished artist, and some of his pictures have a fine dramatic quality, but his depiction of the Swallows and Amazons express the sentimental view of children that was common in the 1920s and 1930s, but would have looked unacceptably whimsical to modern readers.

The proofs were ready for Ransome to correct in June and early the next month he was writing cheerfully to his mother:

I have had a letter from Cape's to say that all goes well with the binding etc., and they now feel that they can count on publishing *Swallows and Amazons* on July 21. I feel quite childish about it, bursting to see the brute and feel it. I haven't been so eager to see a new book since *Racundra* was done.

On July 21 1930 *Swallows and Amazons* was published at 7/6 (37.5p). The print run was 2000 copies – the same as *Rod and Line* that had been published the previous year. W.G. Collingwood was delighted with his copy and promised to buy further copies to give away to everybody. The book's success was ensured, as Wren Howard had thought it would be, by some good reviews, but not all reviewers were

The Arrow with the Green Feather by Stephen Spurrier

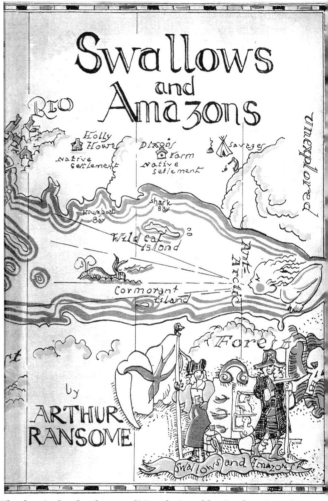

The dust jacket for the 1st edition designed by Stephen Spurrier

quite so generous. An anonymous critic, writing in the *Church Times* said, 'It is not probable that any of the books on our list this week will achieve immortality …'

In his history of the firm of Jonathan Cape, Michael Howard (Wren Howard's son) wrote, 'For Christmas 1930 Cape had one book which held great publishing prospects: *Swallows and Amazons*, the first of Arthur Ransome's series, which in the next twenty years had sold more than a million copies.' Since 1936, when the BBC broadcast a dramatized serial in Children's Hour, *Swallows and Amazons* has appeared at least five times on BBC radio and once on television and a full length audio tape has become available. The book was also made into it a popular film in 1974 that regularly appears on television.

Eleanor Graham, in her article 'The Bumpus Years', recalled the visit Ransome made to the grea

Pearl Fishing by Stephen Spurrier

told him he had to choose between an operation and a protracted cure. He settled for a protracted cure and spent some weeks in Molly Hamilton's London flat in her absence, confined to bed and living on bismuth, milk and olive oil, as well as following his doctor' advice to give up smoking. In September he wrote to tell his mother that he was allowed some toast, so long as he chewed it until it was like cream. It tasted lovely! By the beginning of November he was recuperating at Low Ludderburn when the news came that *Swallows and Amazons* was to be published in America.

In spite of its good reviews, the book sold slowly at first, but its reception had been warm

Oxford Street bookshop where she worked. He had come, he said, to see how *Swallows and Amazons* was doing. Graham told him that it had 'made a good start', but that she was 'sorry that there were no pictures'. Ransome made a 'grumbly sort of pause … they'd take a long time to do. I wondered if he really had any idea of doing it himself … I did not ask the question, but he followed me, and mumbled crossly, "An artist would be sure to get everything wrong." That was evidently more than he could bear. "Good mind to do them myself," he muttered'.

Ransome had been suffering from pain and sickness for some time and was far from well. The doctor whom he consulted diagnosed a duodenal ulcer and

enough for Jonathan Cape to tell Ransome to forget about the essays and write a sequel. His response was to begin a version of *Peter Duck*, which he called 'Their Own Story'. It was not long before he began to have second thoughts and in November 1930 confided to his mother that it would take a lot of working out and he doubted if he would be able to keep it up through 300 pages. The book was to be a combination of fictional fact (the Swallows and Amazons making up a story aboard a Norfolk wherry hired by Captain Flint for the winter holidays) and fictional fiction (their story of the *Wild Cat's* treasure-hunting voyage to the Caribbean). It was not long before he abandoned the attempt. His short draft was published in *Arthur Ransome and Captain Flint's Trunk* and, although it is an interesting false start, the mixture is not a happy one, and only serves to conform that he was right to reject it. Instead he returned to his fictional lake. As he explained to his young neighbour, Desmond Kelsall, the next book would be mostly land-based after Captain John becomes a little over-confident and wrecks *Swallow*. While he was writing *Swallows and Amazons* Ransome had slipped down to Barkbooth to read instalments to the Kelsalls and when he wanted the handwriting of a child for the Ship's Papers, Desmond and his brother Richard obliged by signing 'John Walker' and 'Roger'.

In his first outline for *Swallowdale*, Ransome planned a very different second half of the book. There is no mention of the great expedition to the summit of a mountain – or the Great Aunt. Instead, once they have settled in at Swallowdale and watched the hound trail, Roger sprains his ankle on the moor and is carried on a stretcher made of the Amazon's tent back to the camp. Ransome then explored the possibility of a chase. The notes continue: 'The totem carving ... Offerings ... The Tribe ... The new camp. Titty's cave. The totem taken by the Amazons, The Tribe surround the camp ... They find the Totem gone ......Titty in pursuit. Cairn Beacon fire'.

The notion of a savage tribe and their totem, its theft and the Swallows in full pursuit would be used in *Secret Water*. A beacon fire marking the end of the summer holidays would appear a few years later in *The Far Distant Oxus* by Catherine Hull and Pamela Whitlock, two teenage fans of the Swallows and Amazons, who set their adventures on Exmoor.

Ransome's first intention had been to kill off Old Billy during the previous winter. However, he decided to send him off to the Grasmere Sports instead, and that gave him the opportunity to describe Lakeland wrestling, something that he had tried as a young man. An interesting snatch of dialogue that was never used, shows the more sensitive side of Nancy that would not emerge until *The Picts and the Martyrs*: 'Peggy: "Why did you make Captain John steer her?" Nancy: "Don't you understand you donkey? He's lost his ship, and if I hadn't he'd have thought I didn't trust him with *Amazon*" '.

He began the first draft of *Swallowdale* with relish on 3rd January 1931 and wrote in chronological order, which was not always the case with later books. Ransome set himself clear targets for the writing. By 18th January, he had completed 80 pages, but the diary gloomily records that he was 17 pages behind schedule. He took time off now and again for a little sailing and fishing and he visited Jonathan Cape's Bedford Square premises in March. Cape reported that they had already sold 1,656 copies of *Swallows and Amazons*, which had pleased them, but Ransome confided to his mother that he was aiming for annual sales of 3,000 copies, and until then there was small chance of earning his living from books alone. He also learnt that Cape had commissioned Clifford Webb to illustrate the second edition of *Swallows and Amazons* that they were planning to bring out in the autumn, as well as the new book that Ransome had provisionally called 'The Shipwrecked Sailors' or 'The Camp in Swallowdale'. Webb was a noted engraver, and by the time he visited Low Ludderburn in April, Ransome had almost completed the first draft. Ransome took Webb in *Swallow* to Blake Holme and afterwards sailed round and round while Webb sketched the little boat. Next day he took the artist to Bank Ground Farm and to Peel Island in *Mavis*, and then to the foot of Coniston Water. Ransome and Webb did not hit it off, but Ransome had to admit that Webb's drawings were

Arthur Ransome sailing Swallow 1929 (Courtesy Brotherton Collection)

'really v.g.'. He wrote to Webb praising the proofs of the first set of illustrations, but objecting strongly to a drawing of Titty showing her facing the reader. This conflicted with his own view of illustrations that held the reader should be free to imagine the characters as they wished. However, when he came eventually to illustrate *Swallowdale* himself, his drawing of Nancy in Horseshoe Cove is quite explicit.

There was a break from *Swallowdale* while the Ransomes hired a yacht on the Norfolk Broads. Webb revisited Coniston in May to complete the drawings for the new book, and by that time the first draft was complete. Ransome immediately set out to write a complete revision, and although he had to revisit the

Nancy and Peggy's red caps from a page in Ransome's sketchbook.
(Courtesy Abbot Hall)

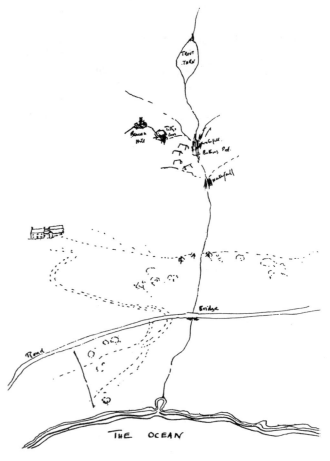

Ransome's sketch map of the Swallowdale country.

opening chapters several times, on 29 July the finished typescript went to the printer. That day Ransome wrote a triumphant, 'Done' in his diary although he was disappointed in the book. Cape had thought that *Swallows and Amazons* was over-long at 352 pages, but its successor was almost 100 pages longer and Ransome feared the publishers would think that it was too long. Ransome was cheered by the news that Wren Howard liked the new book better than *Swallows and Amazons* and he was in a happier frame of mind when he visited his mother at the end of August, so that they could go through the proofs together. 2000 copies were printed in time for publication on 2 November in good time for Christmas.

Shortly before publication, Ransome sent W.G. Collingwood an early copy and he must have been further encouraged to read Collingwood's reply: 'I've been hard at work reading *Swallowdale* ever since getting it and I find it quite as good as *S&A*. I can say no fairer than that. Good luck to the book and its author.'

There were more rounds of applause from Aleppo and urgent requests for the Ransomes to visit them in Syria to see how the children are growing up. Titty Altounyan, then aged 11, wrote:

I have just finished reading *Swallowdale*, and I think it

is just as good – if not better – *than Swallows and Amazons*. I would love to have adventures like that.

Roger can't swim yet, at least not without one leg on the bottom, so if we had a shipwreck, I don't know what would happen. Although I can't imagine how I swam with the telescope. The other day I tried putting both my hands above my head and swimming, but I only went under.

I do hope you will come soon and write another book.

Titty AB

Early in 1932 The Ransomes went to Syria, partly to please the children and to take them a little sailing dinghy. Furthermore, Earnest Altounyan was convinced that he could cure Ransome's stomach problems that had defeated his Harley Street specialist. He was not successful, and there was some friction between the adults, but Ransome was able to make good progress with *Peter Duck*. On their return Evgenia travelled ahead, while Ransome visited Lowestoft to check the accuracy of the opening chapters of the new book. When she arrived home she found that the house had been burgled, and by the time Ransome arrived she was dealing with the burglary in her masterful fashion leaving him to get on with his revision.

Developing the characters of Captain Flint, Peter Duck (based on Carl Sehmel, his crew aboard *Racundra*) and the red-haired boy gave Ransome some fun, but unlike the writing of *Swallows and Amazons*, he had to struggle to complete the book in time for publication before Christmas. Perhaps he was already beginning to tire of his Swallows and Amazons. He did not sail *Swallow* until July, by which time the strain was telling, the stomach pains were still troubling him and he was not sleeping. At the beginning of August he began work on the pictures, as this time the publishers wanted Ransome

SWALLOWDALE

Helene Carter's picture map for the American edition of *Swallowdale*

to illustrate the book himself. Perhaps they had endured enough of his strong disapproval of the work of Stephen Spurrier and Clifford Webb. Figures bothered Ransome, so much so, that he tried using live models whom he could photograph so that he could work from the prints. Colonel Kelsall joined in the fun and constructed a capstan and bunk beds. His two sons Richard and Desmond were the models, together with Peggy and Joan Hudson from Bowness. Ransome thought them 'v. jolly infants' and called the photographs 'hollywoods'. Sometimes of a winter evening he would invite the children to a party in the workroom, where he would issue his guests with penny whistles and fetch out his accordion so that they could sing sea shanties.

At the end of August 1932 the Altounyans returned to Lanehead shortly before the four eldest children were due to start school in England. In September they were all to have raced, but Evgenia noted in her diary: 'Joined in the "all-comers" and last of the season' race on Windermere. Ernest was to have raced Shepherd's *Bittern*, but somehow or other muddled it up and did not get the boat, but took the children on to the ferry landing to watch miserably us sailing THEIR *Swallow*. It was squally and wet and the mast cracked with a loud noise. We hadn't quite completed the first round when the winner passed the finishing line. We got soaked to the skin but it was most enjoyable sailing.'

The year ended on a happy note with the news that *Peter Duck* had been reprinted already and that the American edition would be published in May. 'We shall pull through!' he cheerfully told his mother.

Ransome began *Winter Holiday* early in 1933. From the start he bothered himself about what readers would say when they found that the Swallows and Amazons were not the central characters. He took his usual care with the planning and drew up a timetable plotting the episodes in the story, from the arrival of the D.'s in the north on 11 January, carefully noting that the term should have begun on 18 January, and continuing until they all returned to school on 18 February.

The plot was still worrying Ransome at the end of

Ransome expressed the frustration at being bedridden with his broken ankle in this decoration to a letter.

February, and he fretted that he had not been able to find 'the right scaffolding' and felt sure that there was 'something fundamentally wrong with this story', adding in his diary, 'I doubt if Dorothea and Dick fit this strange tale'

It was at this point that he fell and broke his ankle. The pain kept him awake at night and confined to bed during the day and made writing difficult. He poured out his troubles to his publishers who told him not to worry about the book, because the others had seemed to go through these teething troubles, adding that they liked the title 'Winter Holiday'. Writing to his mother he was a little more optimistic. 'One at least of the two new characters you won't be able to help liking. I find her a most entertaining companion, and in fact I more than half owe my broken ankle to listening to her conversation, instead of watching my feet.'

By the middle of March, continued worry over the book had aggravated his stomach condition, and he consulted Forest Smith, the Harley Street doctor who had put him on the milk diet, told him to put on weight and keep clear of aluminium cooking utensils. Dr Forest Smith replied,

I am very sorry that you are having a relapse. I am sure the whole thing is a vicious circle. Worry and working against time makes the acidity return, this interferes with work and so it goes on. I do not imagine that you have had any return of the ulcer.

There is no modification of the diet that I can suggest. You seem to be taking those foods which do not stimulate acid formation and of course you are taking appropriate doses of your powder.

So sorry to hear about the ankle – that certainly does not help.

I enclose a fresh sedative mixture which might help the general condition. Getting the book finished will do still more good.

All through a very hot summer Ransome wrestled with the revision of his wintry tale with Wren Howard chasing him for the script which he wanted in time to make it Cape's big children's Christmas book. When Cape wanted a descriptive paragraph for pre-publication publicity in early June, Ransome replied that he could do it in one word: 'BILGE'. However, more than a month later he produced a 'false, lying and optimistic blurb'. 'Book no good and will not be done,' he lamented in his diary, while to his mother, he wrote, 'Cape insists on me doing my own pictures. Hell!!!' But not all was doom and gloom. The writer and headmaster, Aubrey de Selincourt sent a very cheering letter.

I feel that I must write and tell you what a delight your three books about Titty and Roger and the other Swallows have given me and my children. Nobody has ever written children's books like that before — I have read a good many and I get so sick of the one eye on the gallery sort of thing that one meets so often. Yours are perfect. All four children, six really, have become part of my household.

In order to save time, the first 14 chapters were sent directly to the printers on 17 August and the rest the following week, after the beginning and then the end had given him sleepless nights. Ransome enclosed details of the spaces to be left for the pictures over which he continued to sweat. Wren Howard did not get a sight of the book until it was in proof! Meanwhile Ransome fumed. 'Blessed if I know what's wrong with it, but I know jolly well something is,' he wrote to Wren Howard on 22 August. 'For goodness sake, have a look at the proofs when they come along.'

Meanwhile he laboured over the 20 full-page line drawings and a similar number of tailpieces. He tried to persuade Cape to allow him to draw on grey tinted paper using process white to represent the snow. Wren Howard noted on Ransome's letter, 'No. Lots of extra expense and our margin is too thin already.' Instead, he urged plenty of strong black drawing. Ransome replied, 'I will bear in mind what you say about covering as much ground as possible with black ink so that aunts and such feel they're getting good value for money,' and 'I am getting more and more disturbed about the pictures. What about Helene Carter? I wonder how much you would have to pay her to justify her coming over from America?' Helene Carter was the distinguished American artist who had produced the illustrations for the American editions of the first three books, and who would, in due course, illustrate the American editions of *Winter Holiday* and *Coot Club*.

In spite of his resolve not to do so, he made the mistake of showing one of his sketches to Evgenia who told him that the legs were awful, the figures were comic, and she could not understand what on earth he had seen that was good in it.

Ransome's gloom was lifted by news of how much Wren Howard liked *Winter Holiday*. 'I am most awfully pleased that you like *Winter Holiday*,' he replied to Howard's praises. 'I felt so hopeless about it for so long that I was sure everybody would feel the same.'

Nancy with the pestle and mortar

Crushing from Ransome's sketchbook, drawn from life. (Courtesy Abbot Hall)

Wren Howard was uncertain about the inclusion of Mrs Blackett in the final scene at the North Pole. Ransome wrote a vigorous defence:

> The case of Mrs Molly Blackett, of Beckfoot, accused of pushing her nose in where not wanted, at the North Pole.
>
> Reasons for her action put forth in justification.
>
> (1) Captain Flint's attitude is too near that of the children to provide sufficient contrast between grown up and non-grown up view of the escapade. And just a hint of the grown up view is necessary.
>
> (2) Mothers will think that it is odd if when Mrs B is actually responsible for the Swallows as well as her own two, quite apart from the Callums, she goes comfortably to sleep in her bed without assuring her own eyes that everybody is really all right.
>
> (3) Children who remember *Swallows and Amazons* will think it odd, remembering that after the storm in that book, Mrs B instantly dashed off to Wild Cat Island with a change of clothes etc.
>
> (4) Ejecting her will prevent the author from sliding gently into the last two pages of dialogue the slight insistences on secrecy, and on Nancy (she and Capt. F had been in it together, so that mutual explanations are barred), which said author can't help thinking are important.

This extract gives a valuable insight into the care and attention to detail that Ransome gave to what was, on the surface, a simple episode. He went on to explain that originally he had written a further dozen pages in which he took the story as far as Mrs Blackett taking the D.'s back to Dixons's Farm and them all leaving for school together.

High Topps by Mary Shepard for the American edition of *Pigeon Post*

Launching *Scarab*. Ransome's completed full-page illustration that only appears in miniature on the dust jacket of *The Picts and the Martyrs*.

On 8 September Ransome sent off the first batch of pictures. 'John is my trouble,' he told Wren Howard. 'In two of my best drawings he has turned into a clumsy lout of seventeen or eighteen. I can't keep him young,' and he invited his publisher in a 'P.S.' to 'Throw out ANY or ALL of course' Much to Ransome's surprise Wren Howard liked the illustrations and proposed to use all but one. 'Hi!' he responded, 'I counted on you to hurl forth the worst of those pictures. There are four or more full pagers that Grays [the printers] are expecting. What about

that niggly one of them being capsized in the snowstorm, with Dick's legs sticking up as he goes headfirst into the snow. My wife says that picture is a disgrace, and that I ought not even to have let you see it. I only let it go because I had nowt better, and because a small girl [Titty Altounyan?] liked it.'

But Wren Howard was not the only one to think well of the illustrations, The Duke of Kent said 'Imagine the effect of testing an author's fitness to publish a novel by insisting that he should illustrate it himself. Modem instances of successful efforts can be seen in the children's books of Mr Arthur Ransome and Mr Hugh Lofting.' The quotation was used on the back cover of later editions of *Winter Holiday*. Ransome wrote to Wren Howard, 'What did Prince say? But whatever he said, the use of it made by you was wholly admirable in browbeating my missis into a kinder view of my illustrator.'

Such was Wren Howard's confidence in the book that he had 5,000 printed in November. By the beginning of December, it was all smiles again. *Winter Holiday* was an instant success and sold 1,500 copies on the day of publication, and a second impression was in the shops later that month. Its author blushed with embarrassment at his publisher's support. 'I say, you really are going it,' he wrote to Wren Howard on 3rd December. 'Today's advertisement in the *Observer* is something tremendous. I couldn't believe it referred to me ... turned pinker than ever when I saw it.' By Christmas 6,000 copies had been sold and all the anguish – for the moment – evaporated in its success that outstripped both *Swallows and Amazons* and *Swallowdale*.

The euphoria was short-lived, for another struggle began when he moved the D.'s to the Norfolk Broads for his next book, *Coot Club*, which arose out of Ransome's own sailing holidays there in 1933 and 1934. The story of bird protection in the teeth of aggressive carelessness on the part of the visiting Hullabaloos who hunt down the young conservationists with their noisy motor cruiser, rings as true today as it did in the 1930s. A new set of characters and a new environment came easily to him. The plot took a lot of working out.

On 2 March 1935 Ransome began *Pigeon Post*, and for a while he wrote rapidly, even reaching a record 13 pages in a day on one occasion. In spite of the time that they spent looking for a new home, the first draft was completed by the end of June. Ransome thought of several titles: 'The Grubbers', 'Grubbers All', 'Pigeon Post' and 'High Topps'. Once again he wrote gloomily: ' ... read it all through. AWFUL. No grip anywhere. Masses of corroborating detail needed. No tension'. And again: 'The whole book is somehow not there ... all but lifeless. I can't *think* of it'. Reading the beautifully constructed plot with its parallel climax and wealth of detail, it is difficult to imagine how much it cost its author, but perhaps things were never so bad as they seemed in his letters or confided in his diary. Those who have recalled how Ransome appeared to them when they were in their teens recalled that everything in Ransome's life tended to be either marvellous or terrible. Letters exchanged between Ransome's mother and other members of the family suggest that they were always concerned about him, particularly about his health.

For once Ransome seems to have shown the first draft of 'The Grubbers' to Wren Howard, who liked it and thought that 'Pigeon Post' was much the best title. Furthermore, he suggested that the pigeons should be brought in more. Encouraged by his publisher's good opinion, Ransome allowed Evgenia to read it. Her verdict that it was not so very much worse than the worst of the others was, by her standards, positively glowing.

But there would be no Ransome for Christmas 1935, as the Ransomes moved to the East Coast and he was occupied with *Nancy Blackett*. Making his new boat ready for sea took up most of his time for a while, and it was not until the new year that he really settled down to try to provide the illustrations for *Swallows and Amazons* and *Swallowdale* that Cape had been urging him to produce. He was also planning *We Didn't Mean to Go to Sea*, so that *Pigeon Post* progressed slowly. In February, he abandoned the book altogether for a while, and wrote 26 pages of the 'seabook'. He began to make better progress once they had transformed one of the bedrooms into a workroom, but it was a poor thing compared with his barn at Ludderburn, and he confessed to being homesick for the north. Once he was able to get afloat mood changed. He made a North Sea crossing in his *Nancy Blackett* in order to check on the plausibility of the unsought voyage, and a number of shorter trips

G. Wren Howard at the time of *Swallows and Amazons*. (Author's collection)

Dear Sir,

We have received this morning a letter from the Library Association, copy of which is attached for your information. Will you permit us to tender to you our sincere congratulations at the distinction which has been conferred upon you.

We are, dear Sir,

Yours very faithfully,

Jonathan Cape, Chairman
G. Wren Howard, Managing Director and Secretary
Rupert Hart-Davis, Director

There were 29 other signatures – the entire staff of Jonathan Cape – from Assistant Secretary to the Tea Lady! The enclosed copy announced that Ransome had been awarded the Library Association Carnegie Medal for the best book for children published in 1936. The presentation would be made in Scarborough by the Association's President, The Archbishop of York, the following June.

Ransome appeared to be as gratified by the response of his publisher as he was by the award and told Cape that he would be sailing in *Nancy Blackett* at the time of the presentation. However, he *did* appear in person, at Scarborough, though the whole affair, particularly the lack of publicity, disappointed him, and he thought they might just as well have sent the medal by post and saved him the journey. When he forwarded the medal to Cape, so that it might be photographed for publicity purposes, he pleaded, 'Please don't bite it or try to bend it.'

Meanwhile, he was hard at work on *We Didn't Mean to Go to Sea*. Many readers believe Ransome's story of the Swallows' accidental voyage across the North Sea to be his best, but it pleased him little more than the others when finished. 'I am very dissatisfied

before settling down during August to make a few revisions and produce the illustrations.

Pigeon Post went to the printers in time for Christmas 1936 and Cape printed 5000 copies and a further 5000 before publication at the beginning of November.

The following February, Ransome received the following letter:

with parts of it,' he wrote to Wren Howard, when sending him the typescript. 'I fear a lot of people will say the thing's too tough for babes.'

His next book, *Secret Water* examines the conflict that can occur between following one's inclinations and being loyal to one's friends. The ninth book in the series, and the fourth in a row with an East Anglian setting, was a thrilling detective story, *The Big Six*. Then came a sequel to the *Peter Duck* fantasy, *Missee Lee,* set in China. It was not until they were living beside Coniston Water during the Second World War, that Ransome returned to his fictional lake country for the last time.

The books had become so popular, both here and in the United States that Cape had almost reached the stage that they could sell all the books they could print. There had been 20.000 copies of the first edition of *Missee Lee*, and Wren Howard was agitating for another book, although he warned Ransome to steer clear of a wartime theme.

In August 1941 Ransome wrote to Margaret Renold with the germ of an idea:

None the less, I am hunting around about [for] a new one, which both Yanks and Cape's want *quam celerrime* [very quickly] Subject I think the Great Aunt of *Swallowdale*. Captain Flint takes Mrs Blackett off for a jaunt abroad, leaving Nancy and Peggy in charge of Beckfoot ...Damned good for them. The GA hearing this writes a letter to them refraining from giving her opinion of their mother but making it very plain, and invites herself to Beckfoot to look after them ... Now then WHAT? Or have you an immense idea of your own?

In November Ransome set down the plot in a little more detail, perhaps for the benefit of his Aunt Helen, to whom the book was dedicated by way of a surprise 'thank you'.

... what is the final way out that must, without doing violence to the GA's character, make her, however grudgingly, go away, before, perhaps the day before Mrs B comes back, leaving a note in which she gives N and P a good character and implicitly admits that Mrs Blackett had done all right in leaving them alone?????

You observe, I hope, that you are being let into the deadliest secrets of the prison house. I don't know how other people make plots. It is my slow and painful method, checking events by characters, and expecting the characters, by being themselves, to produce the events.

I want at the end, to combine with satisfaction that Nancy etc. have come through without disaster, with the realization of the GA's personal discomfiture (though she must be allowed to save her face) and just the faintest touch of pity for her in the hearts of the young savages.

Ransome readily accepted Aunt Helen's suggestion that the Great Aunt should become lost:

The GA has told the children not to go somewhere, and to be back by a certain time. They do not turn up, and she, furious, determines to catch them out. She sends for the man to drive old Rattletrap and sets out. She goes only a short distance when petrol runs out. The man goes back on foot to get a can. She sits fuming. The butcher comes along, going that way past the farm where she thinks they are. She makes him take her, but on finding that he is calling to deliver meat at a house where she does not want to be seen in the butcher's cart, she gets out. Instead of waiting for him, she takes a short cut and gets lost. Is found by an old labourer (? charcoal burner or his wife) and taken to their cottage in the woods. She orders them at once to go and get the car. One refuses to go because unable to leave the other who ill ... The children come home to find that the GA has disappeared. The chauffeur left her in the car, and has found the car with no one in it. The search for the GA ...

Another working note reveals the careful thought Ransome gave to all aspects of his story:

I am a little sorry for the GA, who perhaps realises in the end what is happening, though she does not say so … unless in her letter to Mrs Blackett on departure … a letter which is something of a shock for Nancy. Perhaps this point of view should gradually become possible for the reader … thus preventing the GA from being the bogy she is during the story for Nancy and the others … perhaps Dorothea suspects it fairly early. Is this possible without weakening the mainspring?

The Picts and the Martyrs progressed steadily throughout January and February. In March there was a ten-day barren period in which he was 'irrevocably stuck'. He complained, 'My mucky book has reached page 232 of the rough squish,' and 'I wish I had another wild *Peter Duck* or *Missee Lee* plot. The new book with strictly domestic interest is damnable. I hate it and so will everyone else.' Things were never so bad as he made out in his gloomier moments and he had 354 pages of rough draft completed and had begun the revision by the end of April. In June he told Wren Howard,

But for being held together with artificial pads and props which more or less knock out the sort of exercise I like, I am all right, thank you Picts and Martyrs, however, are all wrong. Position today: first rough draft completed and ghastly. First 100 pages of second draft now typewritten and rather less ghastly. Total length will be as near as nothing 350 pages of my usual typewriting. Usual 20 full page pictures, I suppose. This means a book slightly, though not a lot, shorter than *Missee Lee*.

I am making Dick and Dorothea the main thread, as in *Winter Holiday,* with Nancy working away as the motive force of the messes, seen mostly through their eyes, and the Great Aunt herself looming in the background

seen by the D.'s mostly through the eyes of Nancy, that is to say two degrees removed until just before the final climax. It is a devilish job and is taking a long time to do. It is the sort of thing that simply can't be rushed at. However, there it is, dull and dutiful, plodding along.

The 374 pages of the revision were completed by the end of July. Ransome had learnt from bitter experience never to be around while Evgenia read his scripts, and he went south to Hampshire to fish. On his return to London, he read Evgenia's verdict in Cape's office. In a long letter Evgenia drenched the script with her sternest criticism, telling her husband that he had 'missed the bus' on all counts, She found it dead, dull and worn out and hoped that the paper that Cape had saved for it would be used for reprinting some of the others.

Evgenia had echoed his own thoughts – and a great deal more – and he stopped publication on the spot. There was 'consternation and monkeyhouse' at Cape, for they had all read the script and liked it, and had managed to save enough paper for 25,000 copies.

Ransome wrote to Margaret Renold that he felt as if 'with much thought and trouble I had built a motor car, and painted and varnished all pretty, only to find it wouldn't move and never could.'

For five months Ransome abandoned the book before asking his mother whether he should publish. Her verdict was sufficiently encouraging to make him change his mind and send the final manuscript to Wren Howard, who rushed into Jonathan Cape's office with 'We've got the Ransome manuscript!'

'God bless his mother,' was the reply.

Cape did not bother to wait for the Christmas sales. Instead, *The Picts and the Martyrs* was published to acclaim in June 1943. Cape had enough paper for 22,500 copies and the book sold so well, that in spite of wartime restrictions, it was reprinted twice the following year. Ransome, his mother and his fans had answered 'the critic on the hearth', but it is unlikely that he was ever forgiven.

In the early 1930s Ransome had looked forward to the time when his sales would reach 3,000 a year. In 1945, 50,000 copies of the Swallows and Amazons books were sold! Ransome had indeed provided for their old age. Not without justification has Ransome been called the J.K. Rowling of his time. The plaudits would follow – an honorary MA from Durham University in 1948, an honorary Litt D from the University of Leeds in 1951 and a CBE in 1953.

Chapter Five

Following the Ransome Trail

When trying to find exact locations for Ransome's stories, explorers should refer to both the text and illustrations, for in order to make better compositions, the drawings do not always agree with the text. The drawing 'The Camp Fire' in *Swallows and Amazons*, for example, shows an open space between the camp and the landing place. *Swallow* is clearly visible, yet we are told that trees surrounded the camp. Ransome changed his rough sketch of Titty and Roger paddling beneath the bridge on their way to the discovery of Swallowdale in order to make the figures larger. In doing so he had to alter the shape of the bridge which is no longer semi-circular. Only when Ransome was making the illustrations for *Winter Holiday* and *The Picts and the Martyrs* was he actually living in the Lake District and could draw from life.

There is a wealth of similar locations that could have been in Ransome's mind when he created his Lakeland geography. He chose locations that were characteristic of the area, adding to the difficulty in attributing particular places. If you explore the shores of Windermere and Coniston Water, you will find several possible promontories that might be Dariens and bays reminiscent of Horseshoe Cove. Perhaps the closest we shall come to finding the key to unlocking Ransome's secret locations is by trying to visualise how well he would know the place, and what its memories might hold for him.

Writing in the *Junior Bookshelf* journal in 1936, Arthur Ransome explains:

> The country is the country of my own childhood … Then there has to be a little pulling about of rivers and roads, but every single place in those books exists somewhere and by now I know the geography of the country in the books so well that when I walk about in actual fact, it sometimes seems to me as if some giant or earthquake has been doing a little scene shifting overnight.

Pilgrims on the Ransome trail today will be more likely to be stuck in a queue along the A591, than rattling along the single line to Windermere. The tiny modern station is no longer the same elegant Victorian train hall which was 'nearly filled' by the Ransomes and the Gnosspelius family when they met the Altounyans arriving from Syria in 1932. This is now the next-door supermarket . Nevertheless, as the road reaches the top of the final rise above the station, the view is much the same as that which greeted Titty and Roger arriving by train in *Pigeon Post*. The sparkling water of Windermere stretches into the distance, and beyond the trees on the other side of the lake are the distant mountains. The town of Windermere is not quite Rio. That honour belongs to

Bowness, its neighbour, a mile or so to the south-west. Windermere was built in the middle of the nineteenth century, within a few years of the completion of the railhead in 1847, and this accounts for the harmony of the confident grey-stone buildings that give the place a feeling of unity and solidarity. The Terrace still stands above the station, and looks much the same as it did when Arthur's Aunt Susan lived there and gave him Sunday lunches during his time at The Old College.

St Mary's Church, where the boys from The Old College worshipped, stands not far away towards the northern end of the town. The Old College itself was nearby at the end of Old College Lane. The footpath along which Ransome dawdled listening to the music of the beck when going on a school walk, is probably the Sheriff's Walk footpath which leaves the road to Bowness after about three-quarters of a mile at Goody Dale. The path leads through a wood, past an unexpected waterfall and reaches the road by the lake near to the Windermere Steamboat Museum.

The museum has a unique collection of Victorian steam yachts and among them, tied up to the jetty, is a craft that enthusiasts will quickly recognise as Captain Flint's houseboat. Her long, narrow hull with its clipper bow, counter stern and high cabin roof is unmistakable. Apart from her role in *Swallows and Amazons, Esperance* is notable as the oldest twin-screw craft in the world and also the most venerable vessel in Lloyds Register of Yachts, having been built in 1869, the same year as *Cutty Sark*. She was constructed from the finest iron for H.W. Schneider, who was himself an iron magnate, in order to take him on his daily journey from his pier in Bowness Bay to Lakeside where his personal train took him to Barrow and his ironworks. Schneider lived at Belsfield, the large house overlooking Bowness Bay and had so many servants looking after

his needs that he built two terraces in Bowness to house them.

Also on display in the museum (and on permanent loan) is *Mavis* that was sailed by various members of the Altounyan family until the death of Roger Altounyan in 1988. *Mavis* was restored and renamed *Amazon* at the inaugural meeting of The Arthur Ransome Society in 1990 and some people believe that she really was the original *Amazon*. They must concede, however, that though Ransome's dinghy *Swallow* and the *Swallow* in the story were one and the same, *Amazon* in the story was new and varnished, while *Mavis*, was not new when Altounyan bought her in 1928 and had almost certainly never been varnished. Ransome in a letter to a friend hinted broadly that *Swallow* was wood and canvas but *Amazon* was not.

Sadly, there is no hope of the museum ever being able to display *Swallow,* as she has not survived the passage of time. When Ransome left the Lake District in 1935, *Swallow* was bought by Roger Fothergill, a young *Swallows and Amazons* enthusiast, who continued to sail on Windermere until the start of the Second World War. Nobody has been able to find out anything further, although there has been a rumour that *Swallow* ended her days as a maritime flowerpot in a Windermere garden.

However, the Steamboat Museum really does have another 'original' on show, for the restored *Coch-y-bonddhu* was discovered by some Scottish enthusiasts in the grounds of a Strontian hotel in a sorry state of repair. She was restored by members of The Arthur Ransome Society to full sailing condition and is regularly sailed by members. Unlike *Mavis*, there has never been any move to rename the little boat *Scarab*, although there is no doubt of the little boat's authenticity.

Ransome chose well when he gave the village of

Bowness the name Rio, for in the high season there is dancing on the foreshore and the constant stream of visitors coming and going make it is as crowded as any Rio carnival. Unfortunately, the chemist's shop that had a sudden run on blowpipes, closed years ago, and so did the general store where John bought the rope for the lighthouse tree. Just to the north of St Martin's Church is Lowside, the oldest part of the village. Here there are narrow winding streets dating from the days when Bowness was a fishing village, and next door to the New Hall Inn, the sharp-eyed explorer will spot the old smithy visited by Dick and Mr Dixon to have sledge runners fitted.

My favourite viewpoint from which to see this part

Esperance, Captain Flint's houseboat, lies afloat at the Windermere Steamboat Museum ready to receive school parties and other visitors.

Low Ludderburn today is much the same as it was eighty years ago. The wooden garage that was built to house Ransome's rattletrap car, and pictured on his illustrated card, still stands in front of the barn in which he wrote *Swallows and Amazons.*

of Ransome's Lakeland is Biskey Howe. This can be easily reached by leaving the shops and following Helm Road for a quarter of a mile, past the Windermere Hydro to the top of the hill. Here a sign-posted and a level footpath suitable for wheelchair users leads to a rocky outcrop. From the rocks there is an excellent view across the lake to a panorama of distant mountains, and to the south is the Windermere Ferry and the foot of the lake. There are plenty of seats, and a little exploration will disclose the well-worn steps cut in the rock to enable Victorian ladies wearing long skirts to reach the highest point.

Coch-y-bonddhu spends most of her time on display at the Windermere Steamboat Museum, but is sailed regularly. She is pictured at the Bristol Festival of Sail in 1998.

Down at the bay itself, the prospect of Long Island and the distant wooded shore of Claife Heights that can be seen from the promenade has changed very little since Ransome's day. It is best visited in the early morning before the lake wakes up. With its Victorian steamer pier, landing stages and rowing boats, the place is still the Rio Bay of the books. A short walk behind the large building that has replaced the Victorian boatyards to the south of the bay itself, will bring the head of the lake into view. In the channel between the shore and Long Island are two rocks, the strangely named Curlew Crag and Hartley Wife. Ransome renamed them Hen and Chicken – names that he borrowed from real rocks to be found in the bay south of the ferry.

At the end of the modern marina, a footpath leading off the road, heads away from the crowds to the National Trust property of Cockshot Point. This can be visualised as being the northern promontory of the Holly Howe Bay, overlooking Long Island, with the south basin of Windermere stretching far into the distance. Ramp Holme occupies a prominent position exactly where we would expect to see Wild Cat Island, and for that reason alone may have contributed something to its creation. A little way along the shore of the bay towards the ferry is a single boatshed belonging to the Scott family. It was Sir Samuel Scott who owned *Esperance* in Ransome's time. They moored *Esperance* a little way off-shore and used her as a houseboat. In the boatsheds near the ferry, George Walker looked after racing yachts and kept an eye on *Swallow,* and I understand his grand-daughter carries on the business today.

Another nautical link with the lake that Ransome knew is the 'steamer' *Tern* which still carries her share of visitors on Windermere, just as she has done since 1891 when she was licensed to carry over 600 Victorian tourists. She was refurbished to mark her centenary and looks much as she did when Clifford Webb drew her, although nowadays the vessel is limited to 250 passengers. The tall, thin smoke-stack is misleading, as the vessel was converted from steam power to diesel in 1958. From her deck on the voyage to Lakeside it is possible to have a good look at Silver Holme (or Cormorant Island). The island does not match Ransome's drawing due to its thick covering of trees that have grown since the departure of the cormorants. Another way to see Cormorant Island is by using a public footpath that follows the western shore for a short way. A few years ago cormorants began to roost on one of the islands near Bowness and they have already begun to kill the trees. North of Silver Holme is Lazy Bay, surrounded by trees and quite difficult to pick out. This, of course, is just as it should be if it is the original of Horseshoe Cove. Close to the eastern shore is the pine-covered island of Blake Holme, that some believe played its part in the creation of Wild Cat Island.

Those with their own boats wanting to get afloat

on Windermere will find the public slipway near the ferry a convenient launching place. Unpowered craft can be launched from the western shore (owned by the National Trust) behind the islands, and from the Trust's Fell Foot Park, which is situated opposite Lakeside at the south of the lake. There is also a slipway at the very head of the lake by The Wateredge Hotel. A forty-five minute cruise from Bowness Bay goes round all the islands off Rio and passes through the narrow channel west of Long Island that was chosen by John during the race with *Amazon*.

From the middle of the northern basin of Windermere it is difficult to see anything that resembles the Beckfoot promontory. But the rocky outcrop, just to the south of Wray Castle, can be clearly recognised from a boat hugging the western shore. Since the introduction of the controversial speed limit, fast motor boats no longer roar across the water. Ransome would have been delighted. As long ago as the early 1930s, he was railing in his column in the *Manchester Guardian* against the Board of Trade for handing over the peace and beauty of Windermere to a few rich men in fast motor boats by declining to impose a speed limit: 'There is no getting away from him. One man in a boat moving at 24 miles an hour can, in thirty minutes inflict himself on every other human being from end to end of the lake ... trying with a tremendous accompaniment of noise and thrum to run away from his conscience.'

There is no island far enough north to be Cache Island, but the head of the lake itself is very much as Ransome described it in *Winter Holiday* and *The Picts and the Martyrs*. Explorers must make up their own mind about the site of the North Pole. On the flat grass of Borrans Park, about fifteen yards from the shore, enthusiasts have set a tablet to mark the spot where the dowsing revealed whatever it was that the dowsing did reveal. Above and beyond the road is Ambleside Park and Wanlass Howe where there used to be a Victorian conservatory that looked just how I had imagined the North Pole. On the other side of the mouth of the River Rothay are two splendid Dariens standing at the head of a deep bay leading to Brathay Hall. It is the only deep bay on Windermere or Coniston similar to the one Ransome mapped for Holly Howe Bay, and the little cliffs offer a striking view of the lake stretching away towards the islands to the south.

A short distance up the River Rothay is the bridge used by Dorothea on her way to buy the cookery book in Ambleside in *The Picts and the Martyrs*. Explorers may want to return to Bowness at this point, before heading south in search of the first of Ransome's homes.

Low Ludderburn can be reached from Bowness by taking the A5074 to Winster village and then turning right along the narrow lane for a mile to the River Winster where Ransome loved to fish. The river should be crossed by the ford and the rising road followed for half a mile before taking a left turn for Low Ludderburn. This is the road Ransome 'crawled' along with a broken ankle after his fall. There is a tiny lay-by with space to park one car beside the road a hundred yards or so before the cottage is reached. Low Ludderburn itself is easily found as the name appears on the gate. Outwardly it has changed very little since the time when it was the home of the Ransomes, except that the yew trees have grown and the garden has matured. In February, the orchard is still carpeted with the snowdrops that so delighted the Ransomes when they first saw the place. Helen Caldwell, who lives at Ludderburn, showed me over the cottage with its low ceilings and head-threatening beams. So thick are the walls of the cottage that a small stone staircase was built within its walls. The upper story of the barn where *Swallows and Amazons*

Present-day explorers need to be properly equipped and guided if they are to visit Slater Bob's chamber. The 'On the Trail of Swallows and Amazons' team emerge after their recording.

was written is a large airy room with a fine polished wooden floor that the Ransomes installed. Colonel Kelsall's signal station on the barn at Barkbooth is surrounded by trees less than a mile away, and may be reached by following the winding lanes. We recreated the signal stations when we made our radio programme, and messages criss-crossed the valley once again. While I was at Ludderburn, Mrs Caldwell showed me some of the collection of bismuth bottles that Ransome had bought to ease his internal problems. These had been dumped at the bottom of the garden

'Visitors think gates and walls are just made for them to goggle over,' said Peggy in *Pigeon Post*. We should always restrict ourselves to the role of Squashy Hat and respect the privacy of the folk who live in any of the houses where there is a Ransome interest. Whilst in the area, it might be worth having a look at Town Head (Beckfoot), which is close enough to be seen clearly without leaving the A592.

Ransome's desk, his typewriter and the various keepsakes that he liked to have around him are on display in the Abbot Hall Museum of Lakeland Life and Industry in Kendal. The room, which is laid out to resemble a study, contains many items given after Ransome's death by Evgenia, including some best-loved books, pictures, fishing rods and a chess set.

Two of Ransome's favourite inns, the Hark to Melody in Haverthwaite and the Red Lion at Lowick Bridge may be visited on the way to the rest of Ransome country. The Ransome's final home, Hill Top at Haverthwaite, is a large square house which stands overlooking the Rusland valley. It can be reached from the south by crossing the River Leven at Newby Bridge, turning left and left again after half a mile.

A quarter of a mile beyond Hill Top the road joins

the valley road leading north to Rusland. Three miles further up the valley is Rusland Church, lying between beautiful rolling hills. It is a quiet and peaceful place, and in a corner of the churchyard, beneath the pine tree that Ransome chose for their final resting place, there is a simple stone memorial to Arthur and Evgenia.

We can retrace Ransome's boyhood journey on the wagonette from Greenodd Station, by driving from Greenodd up the valley of the Crake to the Red Lion, the inn where the charcoal burners used to leave new clay pipes for Ransome one hundred years ago. Lowick Hall is only half a mile from the Red Lion, but as it cannot be seen without entering private property, it is scarcely worth a detour. Instead, turn right and cross the River Crake before turning left and following the narrow road to Nibthwaite and Swainson's Farm. Be warned – there is space for only one car to park beside the telephone box at Nibthwaite. Beside the white cottage near the telephone is the tiny bridge that was once hump-backed, beneath which Arthur tickled trout. Swainson's, or Laurel House as it is now called, lies a short distance up the track which leads to Bethecar. It looks nothing like Ransome's illustration, but the rear of the house has a cross-passage like that mentioned in *Swallowdale*. Beside Laurel House the path forks and the right-hand branch leads upwards. After about 150 yards it is possible to look towards the lake and the boathouse where Arthur and his brother and sisters played. Allan Tarn is clearly recognised: a circular reed-fringed pool with a scattering of water-lilies. A little further exploration along the path will reveal the fearsome-looking Knickerbockerbreaker down which young Arthur slid.

A few yards further along the road a public footpath crosses private land to the lakeshore and the boathouse. This is the place where Ransome used to

Ransome's preliminary sketch.

perform a secret rite:

Without letting the others know what I was doing, I had to dip my hand in the water, as a greeting to the beloved lake or as a proof to myself that I had indeed come home. In later years, even as an old man, I have laughed at myself, resolved not to do it, and every time I have done it again.

The Explorers

Do not leave Nibthwaite in a hurry: it is pure Ransome country.

A mile or so up the lake, the road that runs along the eastern side of Coniston Water reaches the shore at Low Peel Near. Here there is room to park, and from the beach nearby we have launched our dinghy on many expeditions to Wild Cat Island. The island itself is tantalisingly out of sight behind two small bays, that some have seen as possible Horseshoe Coves, and the little cliff known as High Peel Near. The land between the road and the shore belongs to the National Trust, as does the island itself, and there are several footpaths leading towards the shore. It is a matter of simple exploration to reach a place where it is possible to look across the water towards the island's hidden harbour and the landing place. On the shore opposite the landing place there is a small beach which makes an ideal place to land for ferrying passengers to and from the island. It was from this beach that Collingwood's youngest daughter, Ursula, swam to the island with the proofs of Ransome's book, *Edgar Allan Poe,* fastened to her head, in order that Ransome, who was camping on the island, might correct them. In winter it is just the place to imagine Dick or Dorothea for a moment, standing at Dixon's landing place at the beginning of *Winter Holiday.*

Peel (or Wild Cat) Island occupies a prominent position on the lake and is a favourite rendezvous for canoeists. Rowing and motor boats may be hired at Coniston where there is a launching site. Unpowered craft may be launched from Brown How and Monk Coniston car parks. Motor boat (What would Captain John have said?) users should be particularly careful if they try to enter the harbour. Once, we had to salvage a party of enthusiasts who had driven their hired motor boat on the rocks extending beyond the western arm of the harbour and stuck fast. They had not read their *Swallows and Amazons* closely enough!

Peel Island is everything it should be – a little rocky paradise with miniature hills and valleys, sheltering beneath a canopy of trees. In the years to come a lighthouse tree, planted by members of the Arthur Ransome Society, should grow to take its proper place at the north end of the island. A matter of real concern is the growing number of fires that are being lit. Some

The Heald. The Ransomes' home beside Coniston Water during the Second World War after they escaped from the bombing and moved north. (Photo: Ted Alexander)

years ago an expanse of heather on the eastern side was burnt and The National Trust has put up a notice forbidding fires. It would be dreadful if some idiot set the whole island ablaze. The Altounyans knew about the danger of fires and used to picnic on the south-east corner of the island, on the top of the rock, well away from overhanging trees, where their fire would be safe.

Further north the road reaches the shore again and

from here it is possible to look back at Peel Island. Explorers should not overlook the steep woodlands on the eastern side of the road. At the southern end of Rigg Wood there are rows of tall larches and among them, almost within sight of the road itself is a very promising igloo. Whether the ruin was once a bark-peeler's hut, or that of a charcoal burner, I cannot say. The ground beneath the trees in the steep woodlands along the eastern side of Coniston is

Children still play at the old stone jetty to which Ransome used to rush to dip his hands into the water to prove to himself that he was really back.

peppered with charcoal burners' pitsteads. Today charcoal is still burned in the area for use in barbecues. Most of the charcoal these days is burned in metal kilns, but there is at least one collier in the Lake District who still burns in the traditional way.

Mid-way along the lake is The Heald, a long, low bungalow of grey Coniston stone with a roof of green tiles from Coniston Old Man. The building is half hidden among the trees and behind a high wall and is not easy to see. When Ransome lived there he owned half a mile of the lakeshore and 17 acres of woodland. 'Your son is once more a lake country land owner,' Ransome boasted to his mother.

A little further along the road are some foresters' cottages and beyond them, a footpath leaves the road and leads into the heart of Grizedale Forest. The path branches a couple of times, but by keeping to the right-hand track it is possible to enter the world of *The Picts and the Martyrs*. Ransome's description of the path is completely accurate '... something like the bed of a dried-up mountain stream, sharp-edged stones and rocks with here and there a tiny pool'. Peggy was quite right about the wetness of the path after heavy rain, and it is easy to imagine old Cook stumbling up, carrying the half-finished apple pie. A beck does indeed cross the path, and just around another bend is The Dogs' Home itself, looking almost exactly like Ransome's drawing. Of all the Ransome locations that I discovered, this was the most immediately satisfying. When I eventually came upon it after several long searches through the forest, an elderly squatter brandishing a roll of bank-notes occupied it, and the place was filthy. Once he had been removed, members of The Arthur Ransome Society cleared the site.

At Brantwood, look for the protruding Turret Room window, or better still, visit the house and try the view for yourself. After passing Brantwood the road reaches the Collingwood family home of Lanehead. Today it has a useful role as an Outdoor Education Centre for Cleveland Education Committee, but the building itself has a detached look and it is not easy to visualise Ransome bouncing along the lane to call up to Dora and Barbara at the window, 'Talking to you is like eating a strawberry ice'.

Bank Ground Farm is halfway down the fields that slope towards the lake. The side of the building presenting itself to the road does not look like Ransome's illustration of Holly Howe. The building is L-shaped and the other wing may be seen at close quarters by taking the footpath which leads back across the fields from the road beside Tent Lodge, a quarter of a mile up the road. Aided by Ransome's headpiece for Chapter One of *Swallowdale*, identification is a simple matter, although in recent years there has been some modernisation of this wing, as Mrs Lucy Batty – the present-day Mrs Jackson – runs a friendly guest house and lets holiday flats.

Before Tent Lodge is reached, the road passes How Head Cottage where the whole Ransome family stayed for three weeks in 1905 at the time when Ransome was in love with Barbara and Dora Collingwood. Tent Lodge itself is worth a second look, as it could very easily have a place in Beckfoot's creation. Viewed from the lake it does have the correct number of windows!

The village of Coniston does not feature in the Swallows and Amazons stories, but The Ruskin Museum should be visited – if only for the wonderful sculpted head of Dora Collingwood by her sister Barbara.

From the village there are several ways to climb Coniston Old Man or Kanchenjunga. I prefer to take the road that starts by The Black Bull and soon becomes a rough path beside the great ravine of Church Beck. Miners' Bridge, where Collingwood came upon Ransome writing poetry, is just above the main waterfall. The valley opens out at this point and a footpath on the opposite bank leads across the open fell to meet the quarry track. From this point it is a long, stony climb up through the desolation of the old mine buildings and spoil heaps to Low Water Tarn.

A longer way that avoids the worst of the old quarries, and follows more nearly the route chosen by Nancy, is to take the road past the distinctive white Coniston Coppermines Youth Hostel. Here, iron and copper pyrites or 'fool's gold' may still be found among the stones and spoil heaps that disfigure, or add interest, to the region depending on your point of view. The path follows Levers Water Beck and passes in front of the youth hostel, shortly after which the half-way camp comes into view. From here, Coniston Old Man, Brimfell (where Roger saw wild goats) and Swirl How form an impressive semi-circle of mountains just as Ransome described.

Kanchenjunga climbers should leave the track to

Windermere. Swallow *and her crew moved steadily southwards over a desolate ocean sailed for the first time by white seamen.* **Swallows and Amazons.**

Levers Water by a wooden footbridge over Levers Water Beck, shortly after passing some mine entrances. From here a level footpath returns to meet the quarry path after passing the Pudding Stone that stands beside another wooden footbridge. The old pipeline running up the fell used to supply compressed air for Oscar Gnosspelius and John (Willie) Shaw's final attempt to mine for copper in the 1920s. The mine was high above Boulder Valley, beneath the shoulder of Brimfell.

Shortly after passing the Pudding Stone, energetic explorers may choose to follow Nancy's probable route straight up the fell until the quarry path is reached shortly before Low Water. Alternatively, after the hard stony climb through the quarries, the strikingly blue Low Water is just the place at which to relax, before making the steady forty-minute climb up the footpath to the summit cairn. Unfortunately, the final part, up which John and Nancy raced, became so eroded that it was no better than a stony trench, and much needed steps in the worst places have been laid.

The Swallows and Amazons were very fortunate to have such a clear day, for only once, in a score or so climbs, have I seen the Isle of Man from the summit. W.G. Collingwood in *The Lake Counties*, says that there were three cairns (the 'old man', 'his wife' and 'his son') before the Ordnance Surveyors built the present cairn. Modern readers may wonder why Titty named the mountain Kanchenjunga. At the time of the Swallows and Amazons ascent, Kanchenjunga in the Himalayas was in the public eye, as there had been attempts to climb the mountain in 1929 and 1930. Photographs of the mountain had appeared in the newspapers. The mountain was first climbed in 1955 by George Band and Joe Brown and another pair, though in deference to locals who believed a saintly deity lived on top, they did not take the final step to the very crest of the summit.

Novice fellwalkers are advised to use the OS Outdoor Leisure map of the South Western Lake District, drawn to a scale of 1:25,000, to wear suitable footwear and to take some additional clothing, as the temperature on the summit can be as much as 10 degrees Celsius below that in Coppermines Valley two thousand feet below. The shortest descent is to follow the Swallows and Amazons example and take the path all the way to Miners Bridge and on to the village.

The *Pigeon Post* country may be reached by leaving Coniston and following the A593 northwards for a mile and a half to High Yewdale. Low Yewdale (or Dixon's Farm) can be seen a short distance from the road on the right-hand side. At High Yewdale the main road passes over Yewdale Beck, but before this is reached a narrow turning leads to Tilberthwaite. Yewdale Beck forms the upper reaches of the River Amazon. The high ground to the west, marked on the maps vaguely as Above Beck Fells or Coniston Moor, is High Topps itself. In order to link High Topps country with the existing Coniston Old Man/Kanchenjunga area already familiar to readers of *Swallowdale*, Ransome had to create his landscape in a mirror image of the real geography.

The narrow road taken by the dromedaries and described clearly by Ransome, is to be found on the north side of the beck. A car may be parked a few yards up this road at Shepherd's Bridge and the route of the dromedaries followed on foot. The road goes up the beck for about a mile and provides excellent views across the valley to Slater Bob's Mine, High Topps and Grey Screes.

In order to reach the places on the other side of the beck, the Tilberthwaite road must be followed as far as Low Tilberthwaite, where there is space for several cars to park near the bridge. The road crosses Tilberthwaite Gill Bridge and passes a whitewashed cottage with a barn over the cow-house, in about the right place for Tyson's Farm, sheltering beneath the fells which rise steeply behind it.

Slater Bob's Mine can be reached by returning along the road for about 200 metres until a path climbs up the fell towards the spoil heaps and old buildings mentioned in *Pigeon Post*. A little exploration will reveal Slater Bob's Mine entrance, or more properly, Horse Crag Level. In recent years there has been a locked gate in the mouth of the tunnel, for the mine was reopened in 1990 and was worked at weekends by George Tarr, who produced floor tiles. This modest venture closed a few years ago and the mine is deserted once more. The tunnel is clear for 160 metres, and on the way it passes through a large cavern or underground slate quarry. It was here the prospectors found Slater Bob at work.

In 1933, after the final attempt to mine for copper had failed, Oscar Gnosspelius set up John (Willie) Shaw to mine for slate in Horse Crag Level. Shaw was working at the mine when Ransome visited the area

The Watch Tower Rock. Claire Kendall-Price and the four explorers gaze into the mist from the top of the Watch Tower during a break in recording.

with Oscar Gnosspelius in search of information on mining and local colour for *Pigeon Post*.

Tilberthwaite Gill is a spectacular waterfall deep in a tree-lined ravine which was particularly favoured by Victorian tourists seeking the spectacular and awe-inspiring. High Topps can be reached by paths either side of the ravine. This whole area is riddled with old mines and is possibly the most dangerous corner in the Lake District. The deep vertical shafts and unsafe tunnels should be given a wide berth, and explorers should leave small children and dogs behind. Having reached High Topps, you will probably find it rather wetter underfoot than the prospectors did during the draught, but it is a wild piece of country and fully lives up to expectations of *Pigeon Post*. From the plateau it is tempting to follow Ransome's example and climb up the slope to Wetherlam and look down on High Topps from above.

Down in the valley, Dixon's Farm (Low Yewdale Farm) may be reached by several footpaths, one of which starts from near Coniston village. The well-known Yew Tree Farm lies close to the main A593 Ambleside to Coniston Road. The car may be parked at the foot of the Glen Mary waterfall, a short way along the road towards Ambleside. Taking *Pigeon Post* and *Swallowdale* in hand, explorers looking for Tyson's Farm will find that they 'cross [the beck] by a little hump-backed stone bridge' and finish up in a 'cobbled yard of a whitewashed farmhouse'. Behind the farmhouse the wood clings to the lower slopes of Raven Crag: '… a wood of oaks and birches and hazels with here and there a pine rose steeply into the sky.' This corner of the Lake District also features in his early story The *Hoofmarks of the Faun* which begins, 'Under Raven Crag in the North Country, there is a grey farm with a huge granary built close under the fell, where the meadows give way to rock and bracken on the one side and deep woodland on the other.'

A glance at the illustration of Mary Swainson darning Roger and, another at the farmhouse will show that Yew Tree Farm doubles as Swainson's Farm in *Swallowdale* and Tyson's Farm in *Pigeon Post*, just as. Long Scars appears as Swallowdale and later as Golden Gulch in *Pigeon Post*.

Returning to the lake, traditional wooden launches, named appropriately enough, *Ruskin* and *Ransome*, cruise to the head of the lake and down to Brantwood and Torver, giving excellent views of Tent Lodge, Lanehead, Holly Howe, the Holly Howe boathouses and The Heald. They also run advertised 'Swallows and Amazons' cruises that provides an excellent way for land-bound explorers to have a good sight of Wild Cat island.

Beckfoot has been variously identified as Town Head, Lanehead, Tent Lodge or even Seven Gates at Ambleside, and no doubt there are others. A mile or so beyond the village of Torver, the A5084 crosses Torver Beck at Sunny Bank and Oxen House shortly before reaching the shore of Coniston Water. It seems to me that the origin of Beckfoot is to be found here, even though the building looks more like Town Head or Tent Lodge. Oxen House is close to the right bank of a little river and 150 metres from its mouth. Like Beckfoot, it is also situated beside a road running near the lake shore and has a lawn running down to its boathouse. At one time there was a stable block across the yard. Further credence comes from its situation. Oxen House lies just across the water from Peel Island, and was part of the boyhood playground that Ransome evoked in *Swallows and Amazons*.

The remaining area that Ransome drew upon for his stories, lies to the west of Coniston Water between Blawith and Torver near Beacon Fell. He sketched out a rough map of Swallowdale, and apart from a little pulling about and simplification, it closely resembles the real geography. 'Beacon Hill' on his sketch map occupies a prominent position and Ransome probably omitted it from the story in order to preserve his secrets, as the curious reader armed with a map of Coniston could readily find Beacon Fell.

A little over a mile beyond Oxen House there is space for a couple of cars to park beside a beck. There is no bridge, as the beck flows through a pipe beneath the road. Until the Civil Engineer's department tarred the road and levelled the bridges, there used to be a humpbacked bridge here under which Titty and Roger could very well have crept. The beck leads to a small bay with one excellent headland – not the Horseshoe Cove of *Swallows and Amazons* – for there is a subtle difference between that and the Horseshoe Cove of *Swallowdale*, with its emphasis on the headlands or 'points'.

On the other side of the road is a large area of open

moorland known as Blawith Fells. Swallowdale lies beyond the skyline and may be found by following the beck as closely as possible. In summer the bracken grows high, and the sheep tracks used by Titty and Roger are tempting, but do not always lead in the right direction. Explorers will not stray too far if they can still hear the sound of the beck and the noise of the waterfall. The lower waterfall fits Ransome's description and should satisfy the most demanding of pilgrims. The valley itself may be

The Ransomes at Hill Top near Haverthwaite

reached by climbing round the right-hand side of the large rock, down which water pours after heavy rain. Less than a hundred metres away at the head of the valley is a smaller waterfall. The floor of the valley is flat, covered with bracken and inclined to be marshy. Apart from having a splendid Knickerbockerbreaker, and Watch Tower Rock, the valley does not fit Ransome's drawing very well and some explorers are disappointed. It is worth remembering, however, that Ransome produced the illustration several years after the book was published. Clifford Webb's drawing has captured the look of the place admirably and there seems little doubt that he visited the place. In my exploration I have walked for miles over Blawith Fells, as well as checking half a dozen possible sites in the area that were suggested by other enthusiasts. Nothing I have seen matches Ransome's text so well, and no nearby waterfall rivals the splendour of the lower falls.

The valley lies in a north-south direction and is called Long Scars on the maps. Perhaps Ransome rotated it through ninety degrees for the sake of simplicity. At the northern end there is a Watch Tower Rock giving a fine view of Peel Island and the length of Coniston Water. The valley was formed by the same fault in the rock that occurs in the hidden harbour on Peel Island that lies exactly in line with the Knickerbockerbreaker rocks. These rocks were of use to Ransome again in *Pigeon Post* where they fit the description of The Great Wall at the edge of High Topps.

Another valley that was favoured by some is Miterdale, ten miles away near Wastwater. However, the body of opinion among enthusiasts seems to have swung in favour of the secret valley that I found hidden among the Blawith fells twenty years ago.

A little over half a mile from Swallowdale is Beacon Tarn (or Trout Tarn), a favourite picnic spot of the Altounyans, who sometimes swam there. This is one of the most beautiful of all the lowland tarns, having a backcloth of distant peaks – Coniston Old Man, Dow Crag and Brown Pike – to the north, and a low skyline looking towards Morecambe Bay to the south. There are several footpaths leading from the road to the tarn. Alternatively, it is possible to reach the tarn directly from Swallowdale by walking west, ignoring sheep tracks and avoiding the boggy ground. The summit of Beacon Fell is a short climb from the tarn and gives an even better view of the mountains and the lower fells to the north-west that Ransome called High Moor.

Some years ago Adrian Simmonds, a member of the Arthur Ransome Society, took a copy of *Swallowdale* and successfully followed the Swallows track from Swallowdale (Long Scars) to the River Amazon (Torver Beck). Simmonds found the jagged rock mentioned near the start of the march without difficulty, but travelling due north through the bracken and up and down sudden slopes, was more difficult, As he neared to the end of the trek, he came across the four firs at Tower Brow, about half a mile south of the junction of the A5084 and the A593. Sadly there are only three Scots pines now, but another piece of the Ransome jig-saw has been fitted into place

A worthwhile voyage of discovery is to drift down the River Crake in a small boat to Allan Tarn (or Octopus Lagoon), as it is impossible to reach the shore of the tarn without crossing farmland. It is a beautiful and peaceful place, and in among the water-lilies and reeds it can have changed little since Arthur and his brother and sisters played there.

Changes in the country about which Ransome wrote will occur from time to time, and enthusiasts will continue to debate the merit of various real locations. How Ransome would enjoy it all! A few things, however, never seem to change. He would not be patient with any of us who go in search of his locations behaving – as regrettably some Lakeland visitors still do – like litter-louts or Hullabaloos: 'The road below this house,' he wrote from The Heald in June 1942, when petrol for private motoring was strictly limited by wartime rationing, 'is a steady stream of motor cars every weekend, carrying people with picnic baskets, who hurl their waste paper into my coppice.'

Perhaps it is a good thing that there are one or two loose ends and remaining mysteries. As Peggy remarked: "It only spoils things to be too beastly clever."

Arthur Ransome, from a pencil sketch by Roger Wardale

Bibliography

Works consulted or quoted in this book:

Ted Alexander & Tatiana Verizhnikova, *Ransome in Russia*. Portchester Publishing, 2003

Taqui Altounyan, *In Aleppo Once*. John Murray, 1969.

Taqui Altounyan, *Chimes from a Wooden Bell*. I.B. Taurus, 1990

Hugh Brogan, *The Life of Arthur Ransome*. Jonathan Cape, 1984.

Hugh Brogan, *Signalling from Mars*. Jonathan Cape, 1997

Dora Collingwood, unpublished journal. Abbot Hall Art Gallery and Museum.

W.G. Collingwood, *The Lake Counties*. Dent 1902. (Revised edition 1932.) (New edition, revised by William Rollinson 1988.)

John Dawson, 'Swallows and Amazons', *Lancashire Life*. September 1988.

Wayne Hammond, *Arthur Ransome A Bibliography*. Oak Knoll Press (USA), 2000

Christina Hardyment, *Arthur Ransome and Captain Flint's Trunk*. Jonathan Cape. 1984.

Eric Holland, *Coniston Copper Mines: A Field Guide*. Cicerone Press, 1981.

Eric Holland, *Coniston Copper*. Cicerone Press, 1986.

Peter Hunt, *Approaching Arthur Ransome*. Jonathan Cape, 1992.

Claire Kendall-Price, *In the Footsteps of the Swallows and Amazons*. Wild Cat Publishing, 1993.

Robert Bruce Lockhart, *Memoirs of a British Agent*. Putnam, 1932.

Pauline Marshall, *Where it all Began* 1991.

George H. Pattinson, *The Great Age of Steam on Windermere*. Windermere Nautical Trust, 1981.

Arthur Ransome, *Pond and Stream*. A. Treherne, 1906.

Arthur Ransome, *The Hoofmarks of the Faun*. Martin Secker, 1911

Arthur Ransome, *Bohemia in London*. Chapman & Hall, 1907.

Arthur Ransome, *Oscar Wilde*, a critical study. Martin Secker, 1912.

Arthur Ransome, *Old Peter's Russian Tales*. T.C. & E.C. Jack, 1916.

Arthur Ransome, *Racundra's First Cruise*. Allan & Unwin, 1923. (Reissued with an Introduction by C. Northcote Parkinson, Century Paperback, 1984.)

Arthur Ransome, *Rod and Line*. Jonathan Cape, 1929. (Reissued Oxford University Press paperback, 1980)

Arthur Ransome, *Swallows and Amazons*. Jonathan Cape, 1930. (Reissued with illustrations by Clifford Webb, 1931.) (Reissued with illustrations by the author, 1938.)

Arthur Ransome, *Swallowdale*. With illustrations by Clifford Webb. Jonathan Cape, 1931. (reissued with illustrations by the author, 1937.)

Arthur Ransome, *Peter Duck*. Jonathan Cape, 1932.

Arthur Ransome, *Winter Holiday*. Jonathan Cape, 1933.

Arthur Ransome, *Coot Club*. Jonathan Cape, 1934.

Arthur Ransome, *Pigeon Post*. Jonathan Cape, 1936.

Arthur Ransome, *We Didn't Mean to Go to Sea*. Jonathan Cape, 1937,

Arthur Ransome, *Secret Water*. Jonathan Cape, 1939.

Arthur Ransome, *The Big Six*. Jonathan Cape, 1940.

Arthur Ransome, *The Picts and the Martyrs*. Jonathan Cape, 1943.

Arthur Ransome, *Great Northern?* Jonathan Cape, 1947.

Arthur Ransome, *Mainly about Fishing*. A. & C. Black, 1959.

Arthur Ransome, *The Autobiography of Arthur Ransome*. Edited and with Prologue and Epilogue by Rupert Hart-Davis. Jonathan Cape, 1976

Arthur Ransome, *Coots in The North*. Edited and with Introduction by Hugh Brogan. Jonathan Cape, 1988.

Arthur Ransome, *Arthur Ransome on Fishing*. Introduced by Jeremy Swift. Jonathan Cape, 1994.

Arthur Ransome, Letter to the Editor, Junior Bookshelf, 1936

Arthur Ransome, diaries, letters and various drafts and manuscripts. The Brotherton Library, The University of Leeds.

Arthur Ransome, correspondence with his publisher Jonathan Cape. The University of Reading Library

Arthur Ransome, early draft for *Swallows and Amazons*, draft for the autobiography, working notes and sketch-books. Abbot Hall Art Gallery and Museum, Kendal.

Hugh Shelley, *Arthur Ransome*. A Bodley Head Monograph. Bodley Head, 1960.

Alfred Wainwright, *A Pictorial Guide to the Lakeland Fells. Book Four The Southern Fells*. Westmorland Gazette, 1960.

Roger Wardale, *Arthur Ransome's Lakeland*. Dalesman Books, 1986.

Roger Wardale, *Arthur Ransome's East Anglia*. Poppyland Publishing, 1988.

Roger Wardale, *Nancy Blackett Under Sail with Arthur Ransome*. Jonathan Cape, 1991.

Roger Wardale, *Arthur Ransome and the world of the Swallows and Amazons*. Great Northern Books, 2000

The Arthur Ransome Society was formed in 1990 and aims to celebrate Ransome's life and promote his work. A variety of meetings and activities are arranged by six regional and overseas groups. Members receive four publications each year and there is a magazine for juniors. For more information, contact the Society: c/o Abbot Hall Gallery, Kendal, Cumbria LA9 5AL.

Index

DISCOVERING SWALLOWS & AMAZONS:
an autobiography inspired by Arthur Ransome's real-life characters
John Berry

Ransome's books were an inspiration for John Berry – he went in search of his hero, finally locating him after cycling 26 miles around the Lakeland fells. Thus began his quest to find the real-life personalities behind the fictional characters – a quest that led to ultimate success, as described by Jim Andrews, a past Chairman of The Arthur Ransome Society: '... a fascinating memoir ... a true story full of humour and verve'. *£8.95*

A LITERARY GUIDE TO THE LAKE DISTRICT
Grevel Lindop

Recognised as a classic when first published, this is a fully revised and updated edition of an essential guide for all lovers of the Lake District. Aimed at both walkers and drivers, literary connections from earliest times to the present day are described in five routes that cover both the National Park and the Cumbrian coast. The guidebook is enhanced by specially-drawn maps and archive illustrations.   *£10.95*

THE BLUEBIRD YEARS: Donald Campbell and the Pursuit of Speed
Arthur Knowles with Graham Beech

Fully revised account of Donald Campbell's attempts to raise the world water-speed record in "Bluebird" to 300mph. Dramatic photographs, including close-ups and shots of record attempts at full speed. Includes recovery of the wreck and the funeral of Donald Campbell in 2001. "It's a damn good read and there are plenty of rare photos." – Focus magazine *£9.95*

LAKELAND CHURCH WALKS
Peter Donaghy and John Laidler

Nominated for Lakeland Book of The Year, 2002, and with a foreword by Simon Jenkins (then of The Times). 30 detailed circular walks ranging from 3½ to 12 miles with alternative shorter options, each starting from a noteworthy church. *£8.95*

LAKE DISTRICT NATURAL HISTORY WALKS:
Case Notes of a Nature Detective
Christopher Mitchell
Winner of the 2005 Outdoor Writers' Guild Book of The Year (Guidebook category)' awards.

18 walks suitable for all ages and abilities with, at every turn, a world of plant and animal signs offering up their secrets. Fascinating facts help you interpret the countryside by looking at the effects of geology and plant life on the animal population of the area. *£8.95*

BEST PUB WALKS IN THE LAKE DISTRICT
Neil Coates

This, the longest-established (and best-researched) pub walks book for the Lakes, is amazingly wide-ranging, with an emphasis on the quality of walks and the real ale rewards that follow! *£7.95*

All of our books are available from your local bookshop. In case of difficulty, or to obtain our complete catalogue, please contact:
SIGMA LEISURE, STOBART HOUSE, PONTYCLERC, PENYBANC ROAD, AMMANFORD, CARMS SA18 3HP
Phone: 01269 593100   Fax: 01269 596116
E-mail: info@sigmapress.co.uk

For the latest news and details of all our books, visit:
www.sigmapress.co.uk